# What Legally Constitutes an Adequate Public Education?

## A Review of Constitutional, Legislative, and Judicial Mandates

by

Martha M. McCarthy
Indiana University
Bloomington, Indiana

and

Paul T. Deignan
Attorney at Law
South Bend, Indiana

535 4

A Publication of the Phi Delta Kappa Educational Foundation
Bloomington, Indiana

Cover design by Nancy Rinehart

Library of Congress Catalogue Card Number 82-81596
ISBN 0-87367-781-1
Printed in the United States of America

This work was prepared under contract with the National Institute of Education, U.S. Department of Education, Contract No. NIE-P-81-0095. The opinions expressed do not necessarily reflect the opinion or policy of the Department of Education. The work is in the public domain.

# Contents            Page

# 4. Federal Role in Defining and Establishing Standards of Educational Adequacy ..........

# 5. Conclusion ...................................... 94

# 1
# Introduction

During the past few years the quest for educational adequacy has become a central theme in school finance reform. Legislatures, courts, administrative agencies, and citizens are exhibiting increasing interest in the *substance* of educational offerings. They view resource equalization among school districts within states as a necessary, but not a sufficient, condition to improve public education. They seek assurance that educational programs are *adequate* as well as *equitable*.

Some recent legislative and judicial mandates have placed an obligation on school districts to provide an "adequate basic education" or "appropriate programs" to prepare students for future adult roles. Yet the precise meanings of these terms remain somewhat elusive. Delineating what, legally, constitutes an adequate education and translating standards of program adequacy into school funding schemes involve complicated political/technical issues. We undertook the project reported here because of the need for a systematic analysis of legal mandates pertaining to these issues.

## Scope of the Study

More specifically, the purpose of this study was to identify and analyze legislative, judicial, and administrative directives pertaining to 1) the legal basis for asserting a right to an adequate public education, 2) definitions of an adequate education, and 3) standards by which to assess educational adequacy. This purpose entailed investigating federal and state constitutions, statutes, regulations, and court rulings as to the nature and targets of the legal mandates. The dimensions of the study are depicted in Figure 1.

### Research Questions

The following questions guided this investigation:

1. What impact have courts had on 1) establishing a person's right to a minimum level of education and 2) identifying the components of an adequate education?

2. How have states defined educational adequacy through legislation and administrative regulations?

3. What types of standards have the states established to assess educational adequacy (e.g., fiscal input standards, programmatic input standards, pupil outcome standards)?

Figure 1

## LEGAL MANDATES PERTAINING TO EDUCATIONAL ADEQUACY: DIMENSIONS OF THE STUDY

**Source of Mandates**

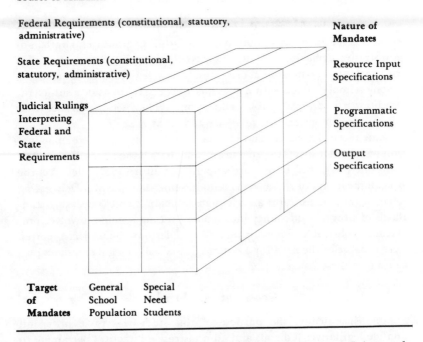

Federal Requirements (constitutional, statutory, administrative)

State Requirements (constitutional, statutory, administrative)

Judicial Rulings Interpreting Federal and State Requirements

**Nature of Mandates**

Resource Input Specifications

Programmatic Specifications

Output Specifications

| **Target of Mandates** | General School Population | Special Need Students |

4.  What role has the federal government played in defining and establishing standards of educational adequacy?

5.  Are there conflicts among the various definitions and standards of educational adequacy (e.g., input, output, special population definitions/standards) that are currently being applied to public schools?

### Procedures

The search for data sources involved two phases. Initially, we conducted a secondary source study to identify 1) related research studies, 2) leads to pertinent state statutory and regulatory material, and 3) individuals with whom to conduct telephone interviews. We located secondary data sources through a systematic review (using key words and phrases) of various library card catalogues (e.g., Government Publications, Law, Education) and educational and legal references systems (e.g., CIJE, ERIC, Index of Legal Periodicals). In addition, our review of *Education Daily* from September 1980 to January 1982 identified recent (possibly unpublished) sources. Also, we interviewed by telephone approximately 10 individuals, identified through the secondary source study as knowledgeable in the area, to ascertain whether we had located all pertinent state statutory and regulatory materials and in-progress studies.

The second phase of the search strategy involved obtaining, reviewing, and screening primary source material upon which most of the analyses would be based. We identified court cases, using the LEXIS computer system, in which the words *adequate* or *adequacy* were used in conjunction with *education, instruction,* or *schools.* Also, our search of the *American Digest System,* advance sheets of the *National Reporter System, American Law Reports, Corpus Juris Secundum, School Law News,* and the *NOLPE School Law Reporter* located cases pertaining to school finance, special-need students, compulsory school attendance, instructional negligence, and competency testing. Initial screening of about 600 cases identified as potential data sources resulted in the elimination of approximately half of them; we reviewed the remaining cases in detail. After locating federal education laws and regulations in the *United States Code* and *Code of Federal Regulations,* we read these laws and regulations, as well as the United States Constitution and every state constitution, in order to identify provisions germane to the topic of educational adequacy. We also obtained and reviewed all state school funding laws and other pertinent state statutes and administrative regulations identified through the secondary source study.

In the analysis phase, we examined all pertinent constitutional provisions, cases, statutes, and regulations to identify 1) grounds for a right to an adequate education, 2) definitions of educational adequacy for normal-range and special-need students, 3) standards for assessing educational adequacy, and 4) translation of program requirements into school funding schemes. Based on this analysis, we drew conclusions about how educational adequacy is being defined and assessed and about the strength of various legal bases for asserting a right to an adequate education under federal or state constitutional and statutory provisions.

# Context:  Definitional Issues

It is necessary at the outset to provide an operational definition of the term *adequacy* and to explain how this concept is distinct from, but intersects with, the notion of equity. The dictionary definition of adequacy is "the state of being sufficient for a specific requirement; lawfully and reasonably sufficient."[1] In court rulings, adequacy has been similarly defined as sufficient, suitable to an occasion, proportionate and satisfactory.[2] Hence, to give substance to the notion of adequacy, there must be a specified threshold level, above which an entity is considered sufficient for the particular purpose in mind.

In contrast to adequacy, equity connotes fair, unbiased, impartial treatment.[3] The terms *equity* and *equality* are often used interchangeably, but equity does not always imply identical or even substantially equal treatment. For example, it generally is considered fair to treat similarly situated persons equally (horizontal equity); however, persons who are not similarly situated may require unequal treatment for it to be fair (vertical equity).[4] Some would assert that equal educational opportunities can be assured only through an unequal distribution of educational resources.[5]

Educational equity can be viewed from several different perspectives, (e.g., taxpayer equity, equity in the availability of resources, equity in programs offered, or equity in educational attainment). The concept of equity is easier to grasp when one is dealing with resource inputs (such as revenues and expenditures) or physical resources (such as teachers and materials). This may account for the fact that so much of the activity to attain educational equity has focused on the inputs of schooling. Equity in outputs (such as behaviors, knowledge, and skills developed through the schooling process) or the broader societal outcomes (such as earning potential) are more difficult to assess and relate to specific school determinants.[6]

It is possible to define the threshold standard of adequacy as embracing the notion of equity; that is, an adequate education might be considered one that is provided equitably to all students. However, equity is not necessarily a prerequisite to adequacy. An adequate education might be defined as a *minimum level* of education necessary to satisfy specified state objectives. Using this approach, a school could be considered minimally adequate as to program offerings, even though the program is inferior or superior to that offered in neighboring schools. Similarly, several schools might offer equal educational opportunities but not provide the minimum education necessary to satisfy the adequacy standard.

The concept of educational adequacy can connote other threshold criteria in various configurations. For example, an adequate education might be defined as one that is *appropriate* to meet the needs of individual learners, suggesting that more than a minimum level is required. Or it might be defined as a *minimum level* of education for normal-range students and an *appropriate* education for students with identified deficiencies. It might embrace the notion of equity up to a certain quantum of education, but allow inequities beyond that amount.

Many sets of actors at state and federal levels are currently involved in establishing the threshold criteria of adequacy for public schools. Indeed, because of the various vantage points from which one can view educational adequacy, different — and at times competing — definitions and standards of adequacy are currently being imposed on schools.

This report is intended to illuminate how and by whom educational adequacy is being defined and what standards currently are being used to assess whether educational programs are legally adequate. Since many of the terms used throughout this monograph are subject to multiple interpretations, we offer the following definitions, which apply unless otherwise noted:

1. *adequacy* - the state of being sufficient for a specific purpose
2. *appropriate* - especially suitable for a particular use
3. *equal educational opportunity* - equitable distribution of educational benefits and burdens
4. *equality* - parity, equal treatment
5. *equity* - fair, unbiased treatment

The remainder of the monograph is organized as follows: Chapter 2 focuses on litigation in which courts have interpreted state and federal constitutional and statutory mandates as they establish a legal right to an adequate education or definitions and standards of educational adequacy. Chapter 3 analyzes state statutory and regulatory activity that directly or indirectly addresses educational adequacy concerns. Chapter 4 explores the federal role in establishing definitions and standards of adequacy for public schools. The concluding chapter includes a summary of the legal mandates and some observations on future legal activity related to educational adequacy.

---

1. *Webster's New Collegiate Dictionary*, (1973), s.v. "adequacy."

2. *See* State v. Davis, 469 S.W.2d 1, 4 (Mo. 1971); State v. Clark, 66 S.E.2d 669, 671 (N.C. 1951); Nissen v. Miller 105 P.2d 324, 326 (N.M. 1940); Vandermade v. Appert, 5 A.2d 868, 871 (N.J. 1939); Commonwealth v. Mathues, 59 A. 961, 970 (Pa. 1904); State v. Bulling, 15 S.W. 367, 371 (Mo. 1891).

3. *See* John Augenblick, *School Finance Reform in the States: 1979* (Denver, Colo.: Education Commission of the States, 1979), pp. 18-20; Norman Thomas, "Equalizing Educational Opportunity Through School Finance Reform: A Review Assessment," *University of Cincinnati Law Review* 48, no.2 (1979): 263.

4. *See* Robert Berne and Leanna Stiefel, "Concepts of Equity and Their Relationship to State School Finance Plans," *Journal of Education Finance*, 5, no. 2 (1979): 111-20.

5. *See* Thomas, "Equalizing Educational Opportunity," pp. 263-67; Allan Odden, Robert Berne, and Leanna Stiefel, *Equity in School Finance* (Denver, Colo.: Education Commission of the States, 1979), pp. 7-13.

6. Thomas, *id.* at 264.

# 2

# Litigation Pertaining to Educational Adequacy: Rights, Definitions, and Standards

A lexis de Tocqueville observed in 1835 that all significant political issues in America eventually become judicial issues.[1] This observation has been verified in the field of education; most school reform efforts have been linked either directly or indirectly to judicial activity. Thus it seems appropriate to look initially at litigation for principles of law pertaining to the issue of what, legally, constitutes an adequate education.

We have reviewed over 300 cases that pertain to some facet of 1) the grounds for asserting a right to an equitable, adequate, or appropriate education, and 2) the judicial role in defining and establishing standards of educational adequacy. All cases reviewed, including those not warranting discussion in the text of this monograph, are listed by topic in Appendix A. Some of these cases, which span diverse issues from civil rights to educational malpractice, are covered in subsequent chapters. The analysis in this chapter is confined to litigation involving challenges to state school finance systems, the rights of special-need students, and compulsory attendance mandates, because these cases have addressed educational adequacy concerns most directly. In a concluding section, we summarize legal principles from these cases and offer some observations as to the future role of the judiciary in establishing a right to an adequate education and in defining and assessing educational adequacy.

## Challenges to State School Finance Schemes

Most of the challenges to state school funding schemes have focused primarily on equity concerns (for taxpayers, students, and/or school districts) and have been based on federal or state equal protection guarantees.[2] However, in deciding these cases some courts have made judgments regarding the adequacy of educational programs and have provided standards for assessing whether a state educational system is minimally adequate. Moreover, in a growing body of cases, courts have addressed the state's obligation, under education provisions in state constitutions, to provide a "basic" or "thorough and efficient" system of education throughout the state. In these cases, judicial interest has focused more sharply on the *substance* of educational programs and the *sufficiency* of state funding schemes in relation to specified *outcomes* of schooling.

Four distinct judicial approaches have emerged in these cases. Some courts have assumed a posture of judicial restraint, deferring to legislatures to determine what educational services will be provided and how they will be funded. Basically, courts adopting this approach have asserted that school finance problems should be resolved in the political arena rather than by the judiciary. These courts have reasoned that education is not a fundamental right deserving of strict judicial protection under federal or state equal protection guarantees. Thus they have concluded that as long as the legislature makes reasonable provision for a minimum education throughout the state, the judiciary should not interfere in judging the adequacy or equity of the program or its funding, even if wide interdistrict disparities exist in available revenues, educational opportunities, or taxpayer burdens among school districts within a state.

A second group of courts has viewed education as a fundamental state right that is entitled to preferred judicial protection under state equal protection provisions. Applying strict judicial scrutiny to challenged school finance schemes, these courts have invalidated schemes that create wide interdistrict disparities due to their heavy reliance on local property taxes. Most of the courts following this approach have focused mainly on impermissible revenue inequities among school districts and have adopted a standard of fiscal neutrality (i.e., funds for education cannot be a function of wealth other than the wealth of the entire state). These courts have not addressed the *adequacy* of the educational programs provided other than to conclude that educational adequacy is related to the amount of money spent. They also have implied that equity among districts in fiscal resources is a prerequisite to educational adequacy. A few of the courts in this second group have looked beyond revenue and tax burden disparities and have addressed other inequities in school finance schemes such as those resulting from special programmatic, student, and school district needs.

A third judicial approach, midway between the two described above, has been adopted by a New York court.[3] Concluding that education is not a fundamental right, the court reasoned that it is a very *substantial* right, deserving of some special judicial protection. Applying this "middle level" review to the state's educational finance system, the court invalidated the funding scheme as not accomplishing the state's objective of providing equal educational opportunities in as nondiscriminatory a manner as feasible.

The fourth judicial approach differs from the three above in that the courts in this category have sought grounds, other than equal protection guarantees, upon which to focus their assessment of state school funding systems. These courts have avoided the issue of education's fundamentality under state equal protection clauses and have based their decisions on explicit state constitutional provisions pertaining to education, thereby not implicating other governmental services in their rulings. By focusing specifically on the state's constitutional obligation with regard to education, these courts have assessed the adequacy of resources, programs, and services to attain desired educational outcomes. Thus they have not been confined to fiscal equity concerns.

In the remainder of this section, these four judicial approaches are illustrated in cases involving challenges to state school finance systems. Each approach offers a different perspective on the right to an adequate education.

### Judicial Restraint: No Fundamental Right to Education

In the landmark *San Antonio Independent School District* v. *Rodriguez* decision, the United States Supreme Court majority concluded that the Texas school finance scheme, with its wide interdistrict revenue disparities resulting from a heavy reliance on local property taxes, did not violate federal equal protection guarantees.[4] Concluding that education is not a fundamental right and that a classification scheme based on property wealth is not "suspect," the Court declined to apply strict judicial scrutiny to the school finance system. Instead, the Court reasoned that because the state school support system was rationally related to a legitimate governmental goal, it satisfied constitutional requirements. The Court held that the Texas state minimum foundation program provided an acceptable means to achieve the goal of assuring "an adequate minimum educational offering in every school in the state."[5]

Despite Justice Marshall's contention that the issue raised in *Rodriguez* involved equity rather than adequacy,[6] the majority concluded that as long as the state has *some* system for providing a basic education for all children, such as a foundation program, the state can satisfy its federal constitutional obligation regardless of interdistrict disparities in school revenues. Conceding that "some identifiable quantum of education" may be a constitutionally protected prerequisite to the exercise of free speech rights and full participation in the political process,[7] the Court declined to elaborate on what this "quantum" might entail. The Court accepted the state's use of minimum school approval standards as evidence that educational offerings were minimally adequate throughout the state.

Regarding the fiscal disparities among districts, the Court majority stated that relative disparities are a legitimate price to pay in order to provide for local control of education. It emphasized that Texas and other states traditionally have made local control an essential part of the provision of educational services. The majority concluded that "in part, local control means . . . the freedom to devote more money to the education of one's children. Equally important, however, is the opportunity it offers for participation in the decision-making process that determines how those local tax dollars will be spent."[8] Assuming a posture of deference to legislative bodies, the majority cautioned that judicial interference in this arena might result in a complete overhaul of state governments, including their reliance on property taxes to support local public services.

Following the rationale espoused in *Rodriguez,* several challenges to inequities in school finance schemes, grounded in state constitutional equal protection provisions, have been resolved on the basis of whether courts have concluded that sufficient fiscal resources have been available for all students to receive a *minimum* rather than an equitable education. These courts have reasoned that there is no fundamental *state* right to an education, and therefore the school finance scheme must only be rationally related to a legitimate state purpose to satisfy equal protection guarantees. Noting that the objective of preserving local control over educational decisions is a legitimate state purpose and that reliance on local property taxes is reasonably related to that objective, several courts have upheld school finance systems despite their resulting inequities. Applying this rationale, the Oregon Supreme Court ruled that the state constitution was satisfied if the state provided for "a minimum of educational opportunities" in all school districts and permitted "the districts to exercise local control over what they desire and can furnish, over the minimum."[9]

The Ohio Supreme Court similarly upheld the state scheme for funding schools, concluding that education is not a fundamental right.[10] The trial court had ruled that the state finance system violated equal protection guarantees by impairing the right of children within the state to attend school in a "thorough and efficient system of common schools" guaranteed by the state constitution.[11] The appeals court affirmed the trial court's ruling regarding the equal protection claim, reasoning that local control was not a sufficiently compelling state interest to justify impairing the fundamental right of students to benefit equally from the state's system for funding schools.[12] Reversing the lower courts, the Ohio Supreme Court held that Ohio's finance formula provided adequate funds for each district to meet the state's minimum education standards. The court found no evidence that any school district received so little state and local revenue that its students were effectively deprived of an education.

The Pennsylvania, Idaho, Montana, Michigan, and Georgia Supreme Courts have taken a similar view in finding no fundamental state right to education and concluding that a minimum, but not necessarily equitable, education must be provided for all students.[13]  In rejecting the contention that the Pennsylvania Constitution requires equity in the distribution of school resources, the state supreme court reasoned that the educational product "is dependent upon many factors, including the wisdom of the expenditures as well as the efficiency and economy with which available resources are utilized."[14]  Also, the Idaho Supreme Court noted that scholars and practitioners cannot agree on whether the amount of dollars available per child is significant in determining the quality of the child's education.[15]  In upholding Montana's foundation program, despite its imperfections, the state supreme court quoted from *Rodriguez* to support its position of judicial restraint:

> The very complexity of the problems of financing and managing a statewide public school system suggest that 'there will be more than one constitutionally permissible method of solving them,' and that, within the limits of rationality, 'the legislature's efforts to tackle the problems' should be entitled to respect.[16]

The Michigan case is unusual in that the governor in 1972 sought and received a state supreme court ruling that the school finance system violated the equal protection clause of the state constitution.[17]  However, one year later, following the *Rodriguez* decision and modest legislative reform to provide a somewhat more equitable distribution in school revenues, the same court vacated its previous order and dismissed the case.[18]  In the latter decision, the court reasoned that its previous interpretation of equal educational opportunities as requiring fiscal neutrality had been too narrow.  The court further noted that significant differences in educational programs between high- and low-revenue districts had not been substantiated.

The most recent state high court decision based on the *Rodriguez* rationale was rendered by the Georgia Supreme Court in November 1981.[19]  Recognizing the direct relationship between a school district's level of funding and the educational opportunities provided for students, the court found "unassailable" the trial court's conclusion that the Georgia school finance scheme is inequitable.  Nonetheless, the Georgia Supreme Court reversed the trial court's holding that education is a fundamental right in Georgia and ruled that the fiscal disparities among school districts created by the dependence on local property taxes do not violate the state equal protection clause. Noting that no taxation scheme is without discriminatory impact, the court reasoned that the school funding program is rationally related to the legitimate goals of providing basic educational funding throughout the state and preserving local control.  While not condoning the disparities among Georgia districts, the court concluded that there is no express constitutional obligation for the state to equalize educational opportunities. Indeed, the court emphasized that since a separate constitutional provision is devoted to education, if the framers had intended to require resource equalization, they would have so specified. Acknowledging that Georgia is unique in constitutionally assuring students an "adequate education," the court found no evidence that the state school funding scheme deprives students in any district of basic educational opportunities. It deferred to the legislature to determine the amount of education that must be state assured to satisfy the adequacy mandate.

Courts in these cases have concluded that the heavy reliance on local property taxes to fund schools, with the resulting interdistrict disparities, is a reasonable means to ensure local control of education as long as the state guarantees that all students receive at least a minimum education. However, the courts have stopped short of defining the "identifiable quantum of education" that may be constitutionally protected. Determination of the components of a minimum, basic, or adequate program has been considered a policy matter that is best left to legislative bodies. These courts have concluded that suits that demand more than a minimal entitlement to educational programs are not appropriate for resolution under equal protection guarantees.

### Strict Judicial Scrutiny: A Fundamental Right to Education

In contrast to the judicial posture in the preceding cases, some courts have not espoused such deference to legislative bodies. Emphasizing their duty to protect significant societal rights and vulnerable minority groups from the overreach of the majority, they have scrutinized inequities in the allocation of governmental benefits and burdens. Concluding that education is a fundamental right and that a classification scheme based on property wealth is "suspect," these courts have applied strict judicial scrutiny to state school funding schemes. The significance of this judicial approach is that when state action affects the exercise of a fundamental right or employs a discriminatory classification that is suspect, the state must prove that it is attempting to achieve a compelling state purpose (i.e., one so important as to justify limiting constitutional rights). Also, the state must show that the methods it uses to accomplish that compelling purpose are necessary, in that there are no other equally effective and efficient, but less intrusive and burdensome, ways to achieve the purpose.[20]

Using this stringent equal protection test, several courts have invalidated state school support systems because of their disparities in tax burdens and educational revenues. These courts have accepted the concept, at least in part, that there is a relationship between the amount of money spent on education and the quality of educational opportunities provided, and they have inferred that equity in the distribution of fiscal resources is one threshold standard of educational adequacy. However, they have not prescribed what kinds of educational opportunities should be provided or what *minimum level* of education must be assured by the state.

The California Supreme Court in *Serrano* v. *Priest* has made the most definitive pronouncement that the state sytem of financing public schools must be fiscally neutral, in that the revenues available for education cannot be a function of local property wealth.[21] While not assessing whether all school districts had *sufficient* resources to attain the state's educational purposes, the California Supreme Court concluded in 1971 that the gross *disparities* in revenues among districts violated both federal and state equal protection rights. The court required the legislature to devise a new school finance scheme that would not tie the availability of educational funds to local property wealth.

In reviewing the state finance scheme again in 1976, the California Supreme Court relied solely on the state equal protection clause because the use of strict judicial scrutiny in such cases under federal equal protection guarantees had been rejected by the *Rodriguez* majority.[22] The California high court reiterated the fiscal neutrality mandate and concluded that the state system still was not in compliance with this standard.[23] Accepting a "distinct" cost-quality relationship, the court held that "equality of educational opportunity requires that all school districts possess an equal ability in terms of revenue to provide students with substantially equal opportunities for learning.[24]

In both *Serrano I* and *II* the judicial focus was on achieving equity in available school revenues, not expenditures. The court recognized that special needs of students and school districts should be considered in devising allocation formulas.[25] While alluding to the apparent deficiencies in educational programs in property-poor districts, the court emphasized that educational adequacy was not the issue before the court. The court's choice to focus on revenue disparities follows a traditional judicial preference to address equity concerns rather than to evaluate whether the programs provided are sufficient for the envisioned outcomes of schooling to be attained. Possibly, the California Supreme Court reasoned that its ruling not only would address interdistrict resource disparities but also would assure educational adequacy in that property-poor school districts would gain the "protection" of the more affluent in terms of their ability to fund sufficient programs. This approach has the advantage of judicial deference to the legislature and/or local community for specification of *how* equitable funding will be translated into an adequate education.

Other courts have followed the *Serrano* logic in striking down state finance schemes because of their resulting fiscal inequities among districts. For example, the Connecticut Supreme Court ruled that the state school finance system with its dependence on local property taxes failed to comply with equal protection guarantees as well as the state constitutional provision requiring "appropriate" legislation regarding the provision of education.[26] The court acknowledged that evidence is inconclusive as to whether increased expenditure per pupil produces better educated students, but reasoned that evidence is "highly persuasive that disparities in expenditure per pupil tend to result in disparities in educational opportunity."[27] The court concluded that property-rich districts can provide more diversity and higher quality in teaching personnel, course offerings, special education services, support staff and services, guidance programs, library resources, and television teaching. It also noted that state standards for evaluating the quality of educational offerings, which pertain to items such as class size, materials, courses, etc., are satisfied more often by property-rich than by property-poor districts.[28] While suggesting that educational programs and services in property-poor districts might be inadequate (measured against state input requirements), the court based its ruling on an assessment of equity — not educational adequacy — among the districts within the state.

In 1980 the Wyoming Supreme Court relied heavily on the *Serrano* logic in striking down the state school finance system as violating equal protection guarantees. The court majority declared that "it is nothing more than an illusion to believe that the extensive disparity in financial resources does not relate directly to the quality of education."[29] Also, the West Virginia high court (although going beyond the fiscal neutrality standard) reasoned that interdistrict resource inequities, which affect educational offerings and outcomes, violate state equal protection requirements.[30]

Several other cases are pending appeal to state supreme courts in which trial courts have followed, at least in part, the fiscal neutrality logic. For example, in 1979 a state circuit court struck down Maryland's school finance plan due to its funding disparities caused by reliance on local property taxes and insufficient state equalization aid for property-poor districts.[31] Concluding that the scheme violated the state constitution's equal protection clause and the provision mandating the establishment of a "thorough and efficient" system of public schools, the court held that the only practical and realistic way of determining and achieving equality is with respect to the distribution of educational funds. More recently, an Arkansas trial court invalidated the state school finance scheme as impairing the fundamental right to equal educational opportunities.[32] The trial judge noted that the funding disparities among districts led to inequities in the caliber of instructional personnel, class size, course offerings, materials, equipment, and facilities. Concluding that the state school finance laws and administrative regulations for funding vocational schools violated the state constitution's education provision and equal protection clause, the court required the legislature to devise a school finance scheme that does not tie resource allocation to local property wealth.

A Colorado trial court has also invalidated the state's heavy reliance on local property taxes to fund public education, concluding that Colorado's equalization aid did not compensate for the wide inter-district revenue disparities.[33] Unlike courts in the preceding cases, the Colorado court reasoned that the finance scheme violated the federal equal protection clause as well as the state constitution's equal protection and education provisions. While applying strict judicial scrutiny only to the state claim (in light of the *Rodriguez* holding), the court ruled that the finance scheme could not be justified even under the rational basis test. It held that the system was not rationally related to the legitimate goal of ensuring local control, as there was no local control in property-poor districts where options for raising additional school funds were effectively foreclosed. Thus the court concluded that federal as well as state equal protection requirements were not met. The Colorado, Arkansas, and Maryland cases are all currently on appeal to the state supreme courts.

Courts applying the *Serrano* rationale have not dictated a particular school finance scheme that the state must adopt. Courts have merely declared that one among many means of financing public schools is impermissible. The fiscal neutrality standard does not restrict state legislatures in selecting from a variety of taxation and distribution schemes so long as the plan chosen is not tied to local property wealth. The judiciary in these cases has deferred to legislative bodies to determine the details of the plans and the level of funds necessary to ensure the provision of a sufficient educational program to all children within the state.

### Middle Level Scrutiny: A Substantial Right to Education

A New York school finance case is somewhat unique in its treatment of education under both federal and state equal protection guarantees. Although recognizing that education is not a fundamental right, the trial court reasoned that, with regard to the state equal protection clause, it was not confined to use of the rational basis test in reviewing state action that affects a *substantial* interest such as education.[34] Applying a middle level test to New York's school finance scheme, the court noted that the classification system used must serve important governmental objectives and must be substantially related to the achievement of those objectives.[35] The court used careful judicial review, rather than strict scrutiny, and concluded that less discriminatory school funding methods were available to the state.

Although using a different standard of review, the New York trial court, like the California Supreme Court in *Serrano*, held that the state finance scheme abridged state equal protection guarantees by denying to students in property-poor districts the educational resources available to students in wealthier districts within the state. The court also ruled that the state constitutional mandate requiring the creation of a statewide system of free common schools was violated in that some districts were compelled to offer an education inferior to that provided by other districts possessing greater property wealth.

In addition, the court addressed the disparate impact of the state aid formula on school districts with special needs. The court held that urban districts, dependent upon the city in which they are located for educational funds, were disadvantaged since they had to compete for fiscal resources from a tax base used to finance a variety of municipal services. While applying the middle level test to this claim under the state constitution, the court held that even the more lenient rational basis test could not be satisfied. One of the objectives of the state's finance system was to reduce disparities in available resources and educational opportunities, and since the scheme perpetuated such inequities, it failed the rational basis test under federal as well as state equal protection guarantees. The state aid formula did not make allowances for the reduced purchasing power of the urban dollar. Moreover, it did not account for the differences in local revenue raising ability per student (municipal overburden) and the special costs associated with educating large concentrations of special-need students in urban areas (educational overburden); it provided proportionally less money for remediation and special-need students to the districts with the highest concentration, highest need, and highest service costs. The court declared: "If equal treatment of unequals is discriminatory, then providing less favorable treatment of unequals has to be regarded as even worse discrimination."[36] However, the court did not specify how the state system should be changed, and similar to the preceding cases, it charged the legislature with making this determination.

In October 1981 a New York appeals court affirmed the trial court's ruling on state constitutional grounds.[37] The appellate court agreed that under the middle level scrutiny test the New York finance scheme unconstitutionally impaired state equal protection rights of students in property-poor districts and in disadvantaged urban districts suffering from municipal and educational overburden. It also affirmed that the finance system abridged the state constitution's education provision, which was interpreted as requiring the legislature to provide an educational system in which all the state's children could be equipped with basic skills necessary to function effectively in society. However, the appellate court rejected the trial court's conclusion that the New York school finance scheme violated the federal equal protection clause. Currently, this case is on appeal to New York's highest court.

## Interpretation of State Education Clauses

Several state courts have used state education provisions in lieu of or in conjunction with equal protection clauses as a basis for assessing the legality of school finance schemes. In these cases, courts have interpreted the state's constitutional obligations and have assessed whether legislatures have fulfilled their duty to define and support the state-guaranteed educational program. This use of educational provisions as a basis for judicial review has some advantages over the equal protection approach. For example, it avoids implicating other governmental services, which is a danger in decisions couched solely in equal protection language. Also, it does not confine the judiciary to an assessment of *relative* adequacy (e.g., fiscal resource disparities[38]), but allows interpretation of the *level* of education required under state constitutional mandates. This approach is not contingent on determining whether education is a preferred right (i.e., fundamental); it is based on interpreting an expressed constitutional directive (e.g., the legislature will maintain and support a thorough and efficient system of free public schools). Thus a court can mandate significant educational reform while staying within its accepted roles of interpreting and enforcing (rather than creating) constitutional rights. Three courts that have based their decisions regarding the legality of state school support schemes primarily on state education provisions have looked beyond fiscal resources to programs and outcomes in defining educational adequacy. Since these cases have provided the most explicit judicial mandates regarding the state's obligation to support an adequate general education program, they are discussed in some detail below.

In the New Jersey series of cases involving the state school finance scheme, a gradual change in judicial interpretation of the state education clause has been apparent. While the court initially focused on ensuring fiscal resource equity, it eventually required program adequacy as measured by pupil performance data. In the original *Robinson* v. *Cahill* decision, the state supreme court, affirming the lower court's decision, declined to base its holding on equal protection guarantees due to the potential impact such a ruling could have on other governmental services.[39] Instead, the court interpreted the constitutional provision, mandating the establishment of a "thorough and efficient system of free public schools," as placing an obligation on the state legislature to provide educational opportunities to equip children for citizenship and employment in contemporary society. Noting that the legislature had never defined the content of the educational program necessary to attain such goals, the court stated that this must be done so that the scope of the obligation would be made apparent "in some discernible way."[40]

The court declined to offer its definition of the nature of the educational opportunities required, but suggested that equalization of expenditures among school districts was a prerequisite. The court stated that it was focusing on dollar inputs because fiscal resources are clearly related to educational opportunities and because the court had been given no other viable criterion for measuring compliance with the state constitutional mandate. However, the court emphasized that absolute dollar equality was not required in that the state may recognize differences in area costs or in the specific needs of students.[41]

In subsequent litigation, the state high court has been called upon several times to assess legislative efforts to comply with its 1973 decision, and increasingly the court has addressed the issue of *adequacy* in educational opportunities rather than *equity* in resource distribution.[42] In 1975, upon reviewing the legislative scheme for the fourth time, the court praised the state department of education's efforts to "establish the components of a thorough and efficient system of education by the formulation of standards, goals, and guidelines by which the school districts and the department may in collaboration improve the quality of the educational opportunity offered all children."[43] The court held, however, that educational guidelines alone, without a redistribution of funds, would not satisfy the constitutional mandate. Thus the court ordered a redistribution of a substantial amount of state aid if the legislature did not develop its own plan within five months.

Justice Pashman, in a separate opinion in *Robinson IV*, asserted that the court should have gone further in imposing a duty on the state to ensure educational adequacy:

> The education clause requires that the state, having chosen to delegate administration of public schools to local school districts, must prescribe statewide standards for the operation of those schools so as to insure that all children are guaranteed an opportunity for an education of a *certain minimum quality*. It must also establish a mechanism for compelling local compliance with such standards, and where, for financial reasons, a local school district cannot comply, it must provide a means for supplementing local resources.[44] (Emphasis added.)

While this was a minority opinion in the 1975 case, it provided the framework for the position adopted by the majority in subsequent litigation.

In response to *Robinson IV*, in 1975 the New Jersey legislature enacted the Public School Education Act with the explicit goal of providing all children within the state "the educational opportunity which will prepare them to function politically, economically and socially in a democratic society."[45] The law provided for a substantial increase in state aid, categorical aid for targeted programs, and equalization aid through a guaranteed tax yield. However, local districts retained some leeway in raising educational revenues within prescribed budget caps.

The act specified the major elements of a thorough and efficient system of free public schools, including adequate instruction in basic skills and creative arts, support services for special-need students, qualified professional personnel, adequate facilities, efficient administrative procedures, research and development activities, and monitoring and evaluation programs.[46] The statute called for the development of state and local pupil achievement standards in basic skills and a statewide system for evaluating the performance of each school. The state commissioner of education was charged with reviewing the results of this monitoring and evaluation system and with directing local boards of education to prepare remedial plans if sufficient progress was not being made toward student performance goals.[47] If a given plan was considered deficient, the commissioner and the state board of education were authorized to direct "budgetary changes" and other measures to ensure that the local school district satisfied the thorough and efficient standards.

The state supreme court assessed the constitutionality of this legislation in 1976. Assuming that full funding was forthcoming, the court concluded that the act was constitutional.[48] Within a year, however, the court rendered its sixth *Robinson* decision, in which it enjoined public officials in New Jersey from expending any funds for the support of public schools (excluding certain fixed costs) due to the legislature's failure to provide funds for the 1975 act.[49] After being closed for one week, schools were reopened because of the adoption of a state income tax to support the act.

Between 1973 and 1976 the New Jersey Supreme Court appeared to shift its major concern from *equity* in fiscal resources to *adequacy* in educational programs measured by student performance in basic skills. In *Robinson V* the court applauded the statutorily prescribed system to monitor school effectiveness in terms of the attainment of pupil achievement objectives. The New Jersey Supreme Court indicated that as long as the state assures that all districts satisfy the thorough and efficient standard (i.e., student mastery of basic skills necessary for citizenship and employment), provision for some local leeway in funding additional programs is constitutionally permissible. Thus equalization of educational expenditures within the state, although the focus of the original *Robinson* suit, has not been judicially required.[50]

Litigation and legislation in the state of Washington also is illustrative of a change in focus from concern for equity in the distribution of resources to adequacy in program offerings. In 1974 the state's system for funding public schools was challenged as failing to make ample provision for a basic education for all children in the state as prescribed by the Washington Constitution.[51] Further, it was alleged that children and taxpayers were denied equal protection due to differences in assessed property valuation per pupil among school districts. The Washington Supreme Court rejected these allegations and held that there was no evidence of a violation of equal protection guarantees. The court relied on *Rodriguez* in concluding that the Washington system of funding schools was a "proper" and "pragmatic" method of discharging its duty to educate the children within its borders. The court concluded that a general and uniform system (as mandated by the state constitution) is one in which "every child in the state has free access to certain minimum and reasonably standardized educational instructional facilities and opportunities to at least the twelfth grade."[52] While not elaborating on the specific components of the guaranteed minimum education, the court concluded that there was no evidence presented that any children were denied such opportunities. Thus the court deferred to the state legislature to decide whether or not to alter the school finance scheme.

Four years later, however, the state's use of excess local levies to generate educational revenue was contested, and the same court interpreted differently the constitutionally mandated "paramount duty" placed on the legislature to make ample provision for a basic education for all children within the state. Specifically, the court declared that students in every school district have a constitutional right to an *adequately funded* basic educational program.[53] Noting that the legislature had not defined the components of the constitutionally required basic education, the court selected three available definitions to use in assessing the adequacy of the state school finance scheme. Under the first definition, a basic education is one that satisfies state laws and regulations pertaining to minimum school inputs (e.g., teacher qualifications, prescribed courses, instructional time). Another approach is to define the basic program in terms of state school accreditation standards. Under the third definition, a basic education is defined by the "collective wisdom" of educators, school boards, and parents throughout the state—in essence, a state norm as to current practices for the "normal range" student.[54] Applying each of these definitions, the court concluded that the Washington finance scheme did not adequately support a basic educational program in all schools.

The court held that the legislature was obligated to identify the specific components of the basic program and to assure their full support from "dependable and regular tax sources."[55] The court stated that, in defining the program, the legislature was not limited to the three approaches cited in the decision. While plaintiffs asked for judicial guidelines as to specific features of the basic program, such as deployment of instructional and classified staff, staffing ratios and salaries, provision of individualized instruction for special-need students, recognition of unique demographical and geographical demands, and use of support services,[56] the court concluded that the substantive content of the basic program should be left to the legislature. Thus, while mandating that the state must fully support a basic education for all students, the court deferred to lawmakers for delineation of the specific components of the state-guaranteed program. The court did note, however, that the state's educational obligation extends beyond mere reading, writing, and arithmetic; it must prepare children to participate effectively and intelligently in the political system and compete in a free enterprise economic system.

The West Virginia Supreme Court also has interpreted the meaning of the state constitutional mandate pertaining to the legislature's duty to provide for education.[57] This court differed from the New Jersey and Washington courts in that it concluded that education is a fundamental right under state equal protection guarantees, thus subjecting to strict judicial scrutiny the state's means of carrying out its constitutional duty to provide a "thorough and efficient" system of education.[58] Declaring that discriminatory classifications in the state's foundation program (not justified by a compelling governmental interest) would violate the equal protection clause, the court went *beyond* the fiscal neutrality standard in interpreting West Virginia's constitutional obligations. It held that provision of a thorough and efficient educational system requires more than equality in funding; it means that schools must satisfy *high quality* statewide educational standards.

The court defined a "thorough and efficient" system as requiring equal educational opportunities in terms of *substantive programs* and *results*, "no matter what the expenditures may be."[59] Such an educational system must develop, "as best the state of education expertise allows, the minds, bodies and social morality of its charges to prepare them for useful and happy occupations, recreation and citizenship," and must do so economically.[60] More specifically, the constitutionally required system of schools must develop every child to his or her capacity in basic skill areas, knowledge of government, self-knowledge and knowledge of his or her total environment, work-training and advanced academic training, recreational pursuits, interests in all creative arts, and social ethics. The court also noted that implicit in this definition of a thorough and efficient system are good physical facilities, appropriate instructional materials and personnel, and careful state and local supervision to prevent waste and to monitor pupil, teacher, and administrative competency. The court interpreted the state constitutional mandate as requiring the legislature to prescribe high educational standards and to evaluate whether such standards are being satisfied in all schools within the state.

The court found that in some counties the schools were "woefully inadequate" under its definition of a "thorough and efficient" system and further noted significant interdistrict disparities in the quality and breadth of educational services. Cited among examples of inadequacy and disparity in resources, programs, and student performance were the following:

1. The facilities, curricula, and other school services are more extensive, diverse and of better quality in the property-rich districts than in property-poor districts.

2. Physical plant inadequacies in property-poor districts constitute potential threats to the health and welfare of students.

3. Property-poor school districts cannot offer the type and quality of educational program offered by property-wealthy districts because of reliance on local property wealth as a revenue source.

4. State aid does not eliminate the disparity between property-poor districts and those with greater wealth.

5. The provisions for special education do not meet the statutory requirements of the West Virginia Code in property-poor school districts.

6. The facilities, curricula, and other services in the property-poor districts fail to meet many standards of the West Virginia Comprehensive Program, the West Virginia Standards for Classification of Secondary Schools, and/or the North Central Association Policies and Standards.

7. The education success rate of the property-poor districts, as measured by test scores or the number of students who go on to obtain additional education or training after high school, is much lower than that of students from districts with greater property wealth.

8. Standardized test scores of students from property-poor districts fall below the state and national averages in virtually every category.

9. The absenteeism and withdrawal rates in the property-poor districts are much higher than in non-poor districts.[61]

The case was remanded for additional evidentiary development to determine whether the inadequacies in some districts and interdistrict disparities have resulted from the statutory scheme for funding schools or from other problems, such as improper property assessment practices or administrative inefficiency. The lower court was instructed to review the state's foundation program, building fund, property assessment system, and state and local administrative practices in making this determination. The West Virginia high court noted that the foundation program may be able to withstand constitutional scrutiny if demonstrated that it makes provisions for supplementary aid to flow to property-poor districts in such a manner that they can meet the requirements of a thorough and efficient system. The court indicated, however, that such a conclusion seems unlikely, given the evidence of glaring deficiencies in some districts. The court also emphasized that it is ultimately the responsibility of the state, not the local community, to guarantee that all districts receive adequate funds to ensure "equality in substantive educational offerings and results."[62]

These judicial interpretations of state education provisions are notable because the courts have addressed the scope of the state's educational obligations and have required legislatures to carry out constitutional directives by identifying the specific features of and quality standards for the constitutionally guaranteed program. Moreover, these courts have not focused only on attaining equity in tax burden or resource distribution (although this has been considered important), but have looked beyond fiscal inputs to the adequacy of program offerings and outcomes. All three of these courts concluded that the legislatures have a state constitutional obligation to provide for an educational system that will at least enable all students to participate in the political system and compete in a free enterprise economy. The legislatures have been required not only to specify what such an education entails but also to ensure its adequate support.

Even though these courts have been assertive in explicating the state's constitutional duty to provide for an adequate, basic, or thorough and efficient educational system, they have been reluctant to prescribe precise input or output specifications for schools. They have deferred to legislative bodies to identify the specific components of an adequate education in settings that presumably are more appropriate for this type of policy determination. The West Virginia high court emphasized that "great weight" should be given to legislative standards in this area.[63] Identification of the features of the guaranteed program requires more technical knowledge than does an assessment of equity among schools. For example, a court can determine if all schools provide students an opportunity to take foreign languages, but the decision as to whether such an opportunity *should* be a part of the basic education program requires substantial professional knowledge as well as public endorsement.[64]

Yet, where lawmakers determine the components of the minimum program using the norm among districts within the state or where such components reflect the strength of lobbying efforts, it may be that the state-guaranteed program is not actually adequate to attain prescribed goals. This uncertainty may be one reason that some courts recently have preferred an outcome definition of the state's educational obligations. If the state is responsible for assuring specific educational results and the state-supported program is not producing these outcomes, a court conceivably might require the legislature to redefine the components of the guaranteed program.

## Rights of Special-Need Students

In the latter 1960s courts rejected allegations that the United States Constitution requires educational resources to be expended according to pupils' needs. In finding such an assertion to be nonjusticable, an Illinois federal court concluded that the Constitution offered "no discoverable and manageable standards" by which a court could assess whether students' needs were being adequately addressed.[65] The court noted that since such needs vary, local communities should make assessments of needs and devise strategies to meet them. It further reasoned that there is no federal constitutional requirement that public school expenditures must be made *only* on the basis of pupils' needs, without regard to the financial strength of the local district. The court concluded that the allocation of public revenues is a basic policy decision that should be handled by the legislature, not the judiciary.

Recently, however, a new wave of educational-needs cases, based on interpretations of federal and state statutory protections, have been more successful. In these cases, courts have assessed whether school districts are fulfilling their statutory obligations to provide appropriate programs for children with certain disabilities. This change in judicial posture over the past decade appears to have occurred primarily because legislative bodies have prescribed standards for courts to use in evaluating program adequacy for certain types of pupils. Special interest groups have become better organized and more aggressive in securing legislation outlining the educational rights of children with unique needs — primarily handicapping conditions. Thus the judiciary no longer is forced to evaluate certain educational-needs cases on constitutional grounds that offer no "manageable standards" for determining whether or not rights have been violated.

Unlike the litigation reviewed in the preceding section of this chapter, these cases have not involved challenges to state school support schemes. Instead, the focus has been on the federal and state statutory rights of special-need students to receive educational services and programs to address their deficiencies. Actually, the initial wave of litigation pertaining to pupils with unique characteristics focused on their rights to *equal* (not special) treatment and was grounded in the federal constitutional principle announced in *Brown* v. *Board of Education:*

Today, education is perhaps the most important function of state and local governments . . . In these days, it is doubtful that any child may reasonably be expected to succeed in life if he is denied the opportunity of an education. Such an opportunity, where the state has undertaken to provide it, is a right which must be made available to all on equal terms.[66]

Courts relied on *Brown* as precedent in striking down various discriminatory school practices and in securing the right of all children, regardless of their disabilities, to have access to the state's public educational system.[67]

It soon became apparent, however, that the mere right to attend school was a hollow victory if some students could not benefit from the educational programs provided. Courts began recognizing that provision of the *same* educational offerings for all students would not ensure equal educational opportunities. Thus the judiciary became involved in assessing whether instructional programs were *appropriate* to address the deficiencies of special-need students.[68] In response to this judicial activity, federal and state laws were enacted to clarify the rights of certain categories of pupils.[69]

Recent litigation has focused primarily on an interpretation of these statutory provisions as to the state's obligation to assure an appropriate education for special-need students. Courts have interpreted some of the statutes broadly, thus placing responsibilities on public schools that are not prescribed specifically in the legislative enactments. These cases have an impact on school finance schemes, because the provision of judicially mandated services in some instances has affected the state's plan for allocating educational funds. Courts have further held that fiscal constraints cannot be used as a rationale for impairing students' statutory rights.[70] Thus the judiciary has not been reluctant to exercise its interpretive powers, even if the court-ordered services and programs have placed substantial new fiscal obligations on the state. A New York federal district court has observed that "only when the financial burden upon the state becomes prohibitive should the court stay its hand."[71] An Indiana appeals court similarly has declared that a desire to conserve state funds cannot be used as a justification for failing to carry out statutory obligations to handicapped individuals.[72]

Litigation involving the statutory rights of English-deficient and handicapped children is particularly pertinent to the topic of educational adequacy because in these cases courts have made some of the most explicit statements as to the components of the educational program that must be guaranteed by the state. The judiciary has prescribed program specifications while adhering to its role of interpreting and enforcing laws developed through the political process. Although there has still been a range in judicial activism, the range has been far more narrow than in the cases challenging state school finance schemes, and judicial conclusions have tended to be more uniform. This has been particularly true as legislation has become more specific in delineating the protected rights of certain types of pupils.

### Functional Exclusion: English-Deficient Students

Recently, the judiciary has been asked to clarify the scope of the state's responsibility to provide special services for English-deficient students who might be "functionally excluded" from a meaningful education without such special assistance. Most of the judicial activity to date has involved interpretations of federal laws and regulations, but since nearly half of the states also have established requirements pertaining to bilingual-bicultural education,[73] state litigation seems likely to increase.

In *Lau* v. *Nichols*, the United States Supreme Court held that under Title VI of the Civil Rights Act of 1964,[74] students with language deficiencies are entitled to special instructional assistance.[75] This 1974 case is extremely significant because for the first time the Supreme Court concluded that there were judicially manageable standards to use in assessing the adequacy of educational programs in meeting the needs of students. The Court reviewed the substance of the educational offerings and placed a duty on school officials to provide special assistance to students with limited English proficiency. However, determination of *what* constitutes an appropriate program under the *Lau* ruling has been subject to multiple judicial interpretations.

Some courts have concluded that bilingual/bicultural programs must be provided for English-deficient students. For example, in 1974 a class action suit on behalf of Hispanic students in New York City resulted in a consent decree, stipulating that all English-deficient students must be provided bilingual instruction.[76] More recently, a Texas federal judge ordered the state to upgrade bilingual instruction and to submit a six-year bilingual education plan for judicial review.[77] The plan must include proposals for teacher recruitment and inservice education, pupil assessment, and the development of bilingual programs at all grade levels. The order stipulates that bilingual instruction must be made available for *every* student with limited English proficiency and must be fully supported by the state.[78]

Other courts, however, have ruled that it is outside the scope of judicial authority to order specific bilingual programs to enforce civil rights guarantees. The Ninth Circuit Court of Appeals noted that bilingual instruction is not the only acceptable way to ensure that English-deficient students are provided equal educational opportunities.[79] The Tenth Circuit Court of Appeals also ruled that such students have a right to special assistance, but not necessarily bilingual education.[80] These courts have allowed local school districts some flexibility in devising the *means* to assist pupils with limited English proficiency, and they have concluded that the provision of compensatory English instruction can satisfy legal requirements.

It might be argued that the courts requiring bilingual instruction have taken primarily an input approach to defining educational adequacy. Applying this logic, an English-deficient child's education would be considered adequate if it entails a bilingual program that meets minimum specifications (e.g., teacher qualifications, instructional time, courses taught, etc.). Conversely, it might be inferred that those courts that have left specific program details for English-deficient pupils to local determination have adopted an outcome approach to defining educational adequacy. Under this approach, a non-English-dominant child's education would be considered adequate if the child masters the English language, regardless of the strategy used to achieve that result.

Although controversy continues over what type of special assistance must be provided, all courts are in agreement that public schools must address the needs of English-deficient students. A Michigan federal court has even extended the right to special language assistance beyond children of foreign origin.[81] The court relied on the Equal Educational Opportunities Act of 1974[82] in concluding that pupils who speak various English dialects such as Black English are also entitled to special instructional help in mastering standard English.

### Handicapped Students: Right to an Appropriate Education

Modeled after federal civil rights laws and regulations that protect the rights of the handicapped, all states have enacted some type of statute or regulation guaranteeing a free appropriate education to handicapped children. Interpreting such federal and state provisions, courts have required school districts to provide a range of services to meet the special needs of physically and mentally handicapped pupils. This litigation is particularly noteworthy because the judiciary has not been reluctant to go beyond the explicit language of the legislation and regulations in placing obligations on public education agencies.

For example, courts have interpreted the Education for All Handicapped Children Act of 1975 (P.L. 94-142)[83] as requiring school districts to provide psychotherapy,[84] catheterization services,[85] and year-round programs[86] for handicapped children, even though such requirements are not specifically included in the act. In fact, as a result of a Fifth Circuit Court of Appeals ruling,[87] the regulations for P.L. 94-142 were amended to specifically include catheterization as a related service that must be provided for handicapped children who cannot participate in the educational program without such assistance.[88]

Courts also have extended the impact of the requirement (contained in federal and most state provisions) that a handicapped child must be placed in a private facility if an appropriate program is not available in the public forum. Public school districts have been held responsible for transportation and maintenance costs as well as educational expenses associated with such private placements, even if in a different state.[89] Some courts have ordered school districts to incur noneducational costs for such private residential placements, reasoning that a handicapped child's educational, social, and emotional needs cannot be separated.[90]

The judiciary also has been active in interpreting handicapped children's rights to be educated in the least restrictive environment. The judiciary has placed the burden on school officials to justify the exclusion of handicapped students from regular classrooms, although substantial expense may be required to accommodate a specific child's needs in the regular school environment.[91] School districts have been ordered to hire additional personnel and provide inservice training in order to mainstream handicapped children and provide them an appropriate education.[92]

Judges have not hesitated to assess whether specific programs satisfy federal and state statutory directives and to order school districts to provide additional services for disabled children. Clearly, courts have entered the "thicket" of determining what constitutes educational adequacy for handicapped students. By ruling that a handicapped child with emotional problems must be provided psychotherapy, the judiciary in effect has declared that an appropriate program includes psychotherapy if necessary to meet the child's needs. Even though most judicial rulings have been narrowly drawn and limited to a particular case, they have often been used as the basis for administrative policies that place new responsibilities on all school districts in fulfilling their statutory obligations to special-need students.

What criteria are courts using to determine whether a given program is *appropriate?* The Eighth Circuit Court of Appeals concluded that if a child's diagnostic team attests that a program is suitable or adequate, even though not optimum, the legal requirement is satisfied.[93] Similarly, a Pennsylvania commonwealth court reasoned that a handicapped child was not entitled to a "more appropriate" program as long as there was professional consensus that a suitable program was being provided.[94]

However, other courts have reached a different conclusion. A Pennsylvania federal district court declared that programs for handicapped students must *maximize* the children's chance to reach self-sufficiency and "ultimately enable them to participate as fully as possible in appropriate activities of daily living."[95] A New York federal district court ruled that services must enable handicapped children to reach their *full learning potential* commensurate with the opportunity provided for nonhandicapped children,[96] and a Kentucky federal court concluded that school districts must furnish the *optimum* in the way of education to those to whom "nature has dealt less than a full hand."[97] Recently, an Indiana appeals court held that a treatment plan, characterized by experts as the *"best possible"* program, was in fact the only appropriate plan, because of the severity of the person's handicap.[98]

There is some sentiment that courts have gone beyond the intent of statutory provisions in declaring that handicapped children are entitled to an "optimum" or the "best possible" program, or to instruction to "maximize their potential." Critics have alleged that the services and programs being judicially ordered to meet the diverse needs of handicapped children are siphoning funds from the regular school program.[99] In 1978 a New York federal district court observed that the federal and state mandates on behalf of handicapped children "may necessitate a sacrifice in services now afforded children in the rest of the school system."[100]

In a recent appeal to the United States Supreme Court, Pennsylvania state officials argued that unrealistic demands have been placed on school districts by judicial interpretations of what constitutes an appropriate program for handicapped pupils.[101] The Supreme Court was asked to reverse a Third Circuit Court of Appeals ruling, requiring the provision of summer school programs for severely handicapped children. In a friend of the court brief, the National School Boards Association (NSBA) asserted that the precedent set by the Third Circuit Appellate Court "affects every school board in the country and could result in a major revision of the very nature of the public educational system."[102] The NSBA also estimated that it would cost $830 million annually to run extended-year special education in this nation. In June 1981 the Supreme Court declined to review the case, thus leaving the appellate ruling in force.[103]

In another case the Supreme Court currently is being asked to review a decision of the Second Circuit Court of Appeals that requires a New York school district to provide a sign language interpreter for a child who was making above average progress without such special assistance.[104] School officials have asserted that the child's educational program was adequate without an interpreter, and thus the appeals court went too far in requiring the school to provide a "more appropriate" program. It has been estimated that the provision of interpreters for all hearing-impaired children in the state will cost $100 million annually.[105] In this appeal the Supreme Court is being asked to consider the massive fiscal implications of the lower court ruling and its potential impact on the general education program. Plaintiffs are seeking clear guidance as to what services must be provided in order for a handicapped child's education to be considered appropriate under federal and state statutory provisions.

Recent litigation, in which courts have interpreted the statutory rights of both handicapped and English-deficient students, has been important in delineating certain components of an adequate or appropriate education for these special-need students. Moreover, the judicial activism in this area — the willingness to prescribe specific programs and services to implement legislation — possibly will influence the judicial posture toward the "regular" educational program. As legislatures and administrative agencies become more specific in stipulating what comprises the basic education to which all children are entitled, courts may play an important role in interpreting such mandates and in prescribing specific programs and services that must be provided in order to fulfill statutory promises.

## Compulsory Attendance

Another area of litigation in which courts have addressed the definition of an adequate education and standards to assess adequacy pertains to compulsory attendance obligations. These cases have not focused on fiscal concerns (inequities or inadequacies) or on the rights of special-need students. Instead, they have primarily addressed the delicate balance between state and parental interests in determining what an adequate education entails.

Some parents have challenged compulsory attendance mandates, asserting that they have a right to provide an adequate, equivalent home instructional program for their children in lieu of public school attendance. Other parents, who have been charged with violating compulsory attendance mandates by refusing to send their children to a state-approved school, have challenged the state's methods of regulating nonpublic schools as interfering with the parental right to determine the adequacy of their children's education. Thus courts have been called upon to delineate the scope of the state's authority to require that all students receive an adequate education and to devise standards for making this determination.

We shall briefly review legal principles from these cases here, because they have implications for consideration of program adequacy in public schools. For example, given that states may and do prescribe more specific standards for public than for nonpublic schools or equivalent instructional programs, it can be assumed that public schools would *at least* be expected to satisfy the state minimums established to ensure that *all* citizens receive a basic education. Moreover, some of the recent suits challenging the adequacy of various alternatives to public education have particular implications as to the state's authority to define and assess what constitutes a sufficient instructional program. To illustrate, some courts have preferred outcome measures to judge the adequacy of nonpublic schools, leaving wide discretion to the schools and parents to determine resource and programmatic inputs. Conceivably, courts could use similar logic in viewing the state's obligation to provide an adequate public education; the sufficiency of the program provided might be judged on the basis of satisfactory student performance rather than by input standards.

**Equivalent Instruction**

Compulsory attendance laws reflect the legislative sentiment that a certain number of years of schooling is a prerequisite—although not a guarantee—of an adequate education. In upholding challenges to compulsory education laws, courts have recognized that states have the authority to prescribe how much education is necessary (in terms of time) to satisfy the state's interest in assuring an educated citizenry.[106] Recently, however, parents and religious groups have become increasingly assertive in challenging the notion that time in school, per se, is a valid criterion for assessing the adequacy of a child's education. In the most notable case, *Wisconsin* v. *Yoder,* the United States Supreme Court ruled in 1972 that Amish children could not be forced to comply with compulsory education mandates after successful completion of the eighth grade, since such school attendance interfered with their religious beliefs.[107] The Court emphasized the unique features of the Amish faith and lifestyle and noted that vocational experiences were provided for Amish adolescents within their self-contained agrarian community. Even though the Court's ruling was specifically limited to the Amish, it might be argued that the Court considered an eighth-grade education sufficient to fulfill state interests.

More common than attempts to obtain exemptions from compulsory attendance mandates have been efforts to satisfy such laws through home instruction. There is a growing home-education movement throughout the country; a national organization has even been established to seek legal support for alternatives to public school attendance.[108] In 1980 it was reported that over three-fourths of the states have some type of statutory provision for home education in lieu of attending a private or public school.[109]

In a recent case, a Missouri appeals court placed the burden on state officials to substantiate that home instruction (authorized by law) was not adequate or equivalent to the public school program.[110] The court concluded that a parent could not be convicted of violating compulsory attendance mandates without proof that "substantially equivalent" instruction was not being provided at home. The court inferred that the legislature should explicate more precisely what comprises an adequate public school education so that the equivalency of alternatives could be assessed.

In December 1981 the West Virginia Supreme Court addressed what is meant by "qualified instructors" under the state compulsory attendance law. In this case the court upheld the conviction of parents for violating the compulsory attendance mandate by educating their children at home without seeking approval from the local board of education.[111] The law allows an exemption from school attendance for children instructed at home if the local board attests that the persons providing the instruction are qualified (even though not certified) in subjects required to be taught in public elementary schools. The court interpreted such qualifications as extending beyond the basic skills to "an instructor's ability to afford students diverse forms of cultural enrichment ranging from organized athletics, art, music, and literature, to an understanding of the multiple possibilities for careers which society offers."[112] Relying on the definition of a thorough and efficient education announced in *Pauley* v. *Kelly*, the court declared that an approved home education program must "develop the minds, bodies and social morality of its charges to prepare them for useful and happy occupations, recreation and citizenship. . . ."[113]

With mounting pressure on state legislatures to allow exemptions from compulsory school attendance for home instruction, litigation involving the adequacy of home education programs seems likely to increase. Courts may require legislatures to be more precise regarding the minimum program components or student outcomes considered necessary to satisfy the state's interest in guaranteeing an educated citizenry.

### Nonpublic Schools

It is well established that parents can comply with compulsory attendance laws by sending their children to a private instead of public school.[114] Also, courts have traditionally held that the state can reasonably regulate such private schools to ensure that an adequate education is being provided.[115] States have varied considerably in how they have monitored nonpublic schools. Some states have required that the schools receive state accreditation and thus satisfy detailed specifications pertaining to items such as teacher certification, course offerings, instructional time, textbooks, and equipment. Other states have not required nonpublic schools to be accredited but have established minimum personnel, curriculum, health, and safety standards for such schools.[116]

Courts in several recent cases have addressed the authority of the state, acting as *parens patriae* on behalf of the state's children, to impose elaborate requirements on nonpublic schools. In two cases, the Ohio Supreme Court has held that the state's minimum standards relating to the operation of private religious schools infringed on the right to free exercise of religion.[117]  The key factor in these cases was the court's finding that the regulations were so detailed and pervasive as to eradicate any distinction between public and private schools. The court reasoned that the extensive regulations eliminated the ability of a nonpublic school to establish its own philosophy, methodology, and curriculum. While acknowledging the state's authority to enact minimum standards to assure that each child receives an appropriate secular education, the court ruled that religious groups must be allowed to instill sectarian beliefs without unreasonable governmental interference.

In 1979 the Kentucky Supreme Court added legal support to the movement to obtain autonomy for religious academies by holding that the state could not require nonpublic schools to meet state accreditation standards, employ certified teachers, or use prescribed textbooks.[118] The court reasoned that such regulations applied to private schools violated the state constitutional prohibition against compelling parents to send their children to a school to which they may be conscientiously opposed.  If the legislature desires to monitor the *adequacy* of the secular instruction in nonpublic schools, the court suggested that it may do so by establishing an appropriate standardized achievement testing program. Where test results show that a nonpublic school has failed to provide an adequate education, then the state can initiate proceedings to close the school. In effect, this court reasoned that as long as a nonpublic school can demonstrate an acceptable output in terms of pupil achievement, the state cannot prescribe minimum inputs to assure adequacy. In 1980 the United States Supreme Court declined to review this case, thus leaving the Kentucky Supreme Court's decision in force.

However, courts have not spoken in unison as to the state's authority to regulate nonpublic schools.  The North Dakota Supreme Court recently upheld minimum state standards for private schools pertaining to teacher certification, prescribed courses, and health and safety requirements.[119]  Similarly, in 1981 the Nebraska Supreme Court ruled that nonpublic schools do not have a right to be completely "unfettered by reasonable government regulations as to the quality of education furnished."[120]  The court reasoned there is a compelling governmental interest that justifies the imposition of minimum standards on nonpublic schools and their personnel.  On the first day of its 1981 October term, the United States Supreme Court dismissed an appeal of the Nebraska high court ruling.

Since the Supreme Court has not yet rendered an opinion pertaining to the regulation of private schools, the scope of the state's authority to monitor secular educational offerings to ensure an educated citizenry remains unclear. While some minimum input requirements for nonpublic schools have been judicially endorsed, at least one state supreme court recently has suggested that the adequacy of nonpublic school programs should be gauged primarily in terms of their output. That is, as long as pupils perform well on achievement tests, state input and program requirements should be relaxed.[121] It might be asserted that if the state's interest in ensuring an educated citizenry is satisfied in relation to private schools by evidence of successful pupil performance, then similar output standards should be applied to public schools, leaving program decisions to local communities. Such an approach would differ significantly from the current norm for assessing the adequacy of public school programs, which essentially consists of compliance with state input requirements.

Another more subtle implication of this litigation pertains to the state's *parens patriae* role to prescribe standards of educational adequacy and monitor compliance with such standards in both public and private schools. The movement to deregulate nonpublic schools has gained momentum, and some of the arguments being raised might similarly be used in connection with public education. Parents might contest the proliferation of state input requirements being applied to public schools (e.g., specified percentages of instructional time devoted to various subjects, prescribed textbooks, designated pupil-teacher ratios) as interfering with parental rights to have some voice in making curricular decisions. Conceivably, one might assert that state-prescribed program specifications accompanying state aid should be reduced to allow more local discretion in determining *how* to deliver educational services. Following this argument to its logical conclusion, school effectiveness as well as the state's fulfillment of its educational obligation would be judged on the basis of student performance.

## Current Judicial Posture and Future Directions

The judiciary has played and is likely to continue to play an important role in educational reform efforts. Courts not only have focused public attention on school inequities and inadequacies, they also have required some legislatures to define the components of an adequate education and to assure its full support. In this section we summarize major points from the litigation review and offer a few observations on the future role of the judiciary in assuring educational adequacy.

### Current Judicial Posture

The United States Supreme Court has inferred that, under the equal protection clause of the Fourteenth Amendment, students have a right to *some education,* even though equity in school resources and offerings is not required. Federal equal protection guarantees have appeared most viable in challenging the total *exclusion* of certain students from school or the *misclassification* of pupils.[122]

The federal judiciary has deferred to state legislatures to determine how much education is "enough" and has upheld the use of minimum state input standards as an appropriate means to assure a basic education for all pupils. Federal courts also have shown great respect for local control in education, including some control over the amount of money spent on local schools. Several state courts have followed the federal lead in addressing the legislature's obligation in regard to education under state equal protection provisions. These courts have concluded that the state is required to assure only a *minimum* — not an equitable — education for all students, and they have deferred to legislatures to determine what the minimum program entails. In some states, legislative discretion is considered so broad that the continued reliance on local property taxes to fund schools has been upheld, despite significant interdistrict disparities in tax burden, revenues, expenditures, programs, or pupil outcomes.

In other states, however, courts have concluded that because of the importance of education to the individual and the state, the adequacy of a child's education cannot be a function of local property wealth. They have defined educational adequacy primarily in terms of fiscal resources and have accepted the premise that a relationship exists between the *quality* and *cost* of a child's education. These courts have focused on impermissible resource disparities among districts and have not defined the *level* of education that must be provided.

A few courts have viewed the state's obligation to provide an adequate education from the perspective of pupil outcomes, such as sufficient instruction to prepare individuals to function as citizens and competitors in the marketplace. These courts have emphasized the legislature's state constitutional obligation to define and support the components of an educational program necessary to attain these goals. Also, in some cases involving the state's authority to regulate alternatives to public education, courts have favored an outcome approach (i.e., student achievement) in defining the adequacy of educational offerings.

While many courts have been reluctant to interpret broadly the state's constitutional obligations to ensure educational adequacy, the judiciary has been less hesitant to interpret legislative enactments. Courts in general have been more willing to review allegations of statutory violations than to create new interpretations of constitutional provisions. Once lawmakers have specified educational rights and accompanying state responsibilities, courts have given substance to vague statutory language and have assessed whether specific educational offerings satisfy the statutory directives. Illustrative is the litigation pertaining to the educational rights of handicapped children in which courts have ruled that particular programs must be provided in order to fulfill federal and state statutory requirements for the provision of appropriate programs for such children. Some courts have placed substantial fiscal obligations on education agencies by delineating the specific services that are required to carry out statutory mandates.

**Future Directions**

It appears likely that litigation dealing with educational adequacy concerns will take place primarily in state courts in the future with the exception of cases pertaining to the federal rights of special-need students. Federal constitutional grounds for asserting a right to an adequate education are problematic because there is no explicit constitutional language pertaining to education. Although there is some sentiment that the due process clause of the Fourteenth Amendment holds promise for attacking educational inequities and inadequacies, this legal theory has not yet been tested.[123]

In contrast to the U.S. Constitution, all state constitutions do contain specific provisions pertaining to legislative responsibility to provide public education, and litigation interpreting such provisions seems likely to escalate. A majority of the states include one or more of the terms *adequate, suitable, efficient, uniform,* and *thorough* in their constitutional mandates pertaining to education (see Appendix B). Possibly other state courts will follow the lead of New Jersey, Washington, and West Virginia in interpreting the scope of the state's responsibilities under these mandates. Such provisions, if interpreted broadly, could become the basis for massive judicial intervention in the internal operations of schools. For example, courts might require legislatures to put in operation vague constitutional directives (e.g., "the state legislature shall provide educational opportunities that the needs of the people may require") by specifying *what* needs must be addressed and to *what level* they must be met. The judiciary might then review the legislation to ensure that it contains reasonable and sufficient means to meet the constitutional obligations.

If additional courts do require legislatures to specify the features of the minimum education that must be assured state support, suits challenging interdistrict fiscal inequities will probably be affected. While the *Rodriguez* majority concluded that no evidence was presented to substantiate that the fiscal disparities among Texas districts resulted in the denial of a *minimum education* to any student,[124] such evidence may be available in future cases. If legislatures define more precisely what constitutes the minimum education that is necessary (in terms of resources, programs, and outcomes) to achieve state goals, courts may have concrete criteria to use in judging whether the programs offered in some districts are deficient and whether such inadequacies result from the state school support system.[125]

It appears that the major judicial contribution to ensuring educational adequacy will consist of delineating the legislature's constitutional obligations and reviewing statutory enactments to ensure that such obligations have been satisfied. If legislation is couched in vague language, the judiciary may interpret the mandates as placing more responsibilities on the public school than were actually intended by the lawmakers. Indeed, judicial discretion is being indirectly encouraged by the ambiguity contained in some legislative enactments. For example, if a state law prescribes that educational programs should prepare students for employment, a court may be inclined to prescribe *what* specific programs and services must be provided in order to implement the statute. Van Geel has suggested that courts may move into the domain of not only identifying what types of educational programs are necessary to prepare students for adult roles but also what specific skills must be taught.[126] As long as there is a gap between legislative promises for education and the means provided to realize those promises, state legislatures may be inviting judicial intervention in the educational policy area.

Will courts become assertive in identifying the *specific features* of an adequate education? Is the judiciary the appropriate branch of government to make such technical decisions, or should issues involving large-scale social change be left to legislatures? Is judicial intervention necessary because of the inaction of other branches of government? Justices themselves do not agree on these questions. Some believe the courts should play an activist role; others feel that they should adopt a position of restraint in this arena.

Even with the most assertive exercise of judicial interpretive powers, however, the responsibility to give "specific, substantive content" to the state-guaranteed adequate education remains with the legislature.[127] Accordingly, the major efforts to define and establish standards of educational adequacy seem likely to take place in legislative forums. In the next chapter we examine state statutory and regulatory activity in this area.

1. Alexis de Tocqueville, *Democracy in America*, vol. 1 (New York: Alfred A. Knopf, 1945), p. 280.

2. Cases focusing primarily on taxpayer equity issues and fees for public school textbooks and tuition are not discussed in the text of this monograph as they relate only tangentially to the thrust of the investigation. However, representative cases pertaining to these topics are listed in Appendix A.

3. Board of Educ., Levittown Union Free School Dist., Nassau County v. Nyquist, 408 N.Y.S. 2d 606 (Sup. Ct., Nassau County, 1978), *aff'd. as modified,* 443 N.Y.S. 2d 843 (App. Div. 1981).

4. San Antonio, Independent School Dist. v. Rodriguez, 411 U.S. 1 (1973) [hereinafter cited as Rodriguez].

5. *Id.* at 45.

6. *Id.* at 72-82 (Marshall, J., dissenting). He also questioned the majority's conclusion that the Texas minimum foundation program guaranteed an adequate education for every child (pp. 86-87), and drew attention to the problem of assessing what is "enough" education to satisfy constitutional guarantees (pp. 89-90).

7. *Id.* at 36-37.

8. *Id.* at 50.

9. Olsen v. State of Oregon, 554 P.2d 139, 148 (Or. 1976).

10. Board of Educ. of the City School Dist. of the City of Cincinnati v. Walter, 390 N.E.2d 812 (Ohio 1979), *cert. denied,* 444 U.S. 1015 (1980).

11. Board of Educ. v. Walter, No. A760275 (Ohio C.P., Hamilton County, 1977).

12. Board of Educ. v. Walter, 10 Ohio Op. 3d 26 (Ct. App. 1978).

13. *See* McDaniel v. Thomas, 285 S.E.2d 156 (Ga. 1981); Danson v. Casey, 399 A.2d 360 (Pa. 1979); Thompson v. Engelking, 537 P.2d 635 (Idaho 1975); Woodahl v. Straub, 520 P.2d 776 (Mont. 1974); Milliken v. Green, 212 N.W.2d 711 (Mich. 1973). Also, the Arizona Supreme Court in Shofstall v. Hollins, 515 P.2d 590 (Ariz. 1973), held that as long as the funding system meets the mandates of the state's constitution (i.e., uniform, free, available to all persons aged six to 21, and open a minimum of six months per year), the system need otherwise be only rational, reasonable and neither discriminatory nor capricious. The Arizona case is unique in that the court exhibited judicial restraint even though it found education to be a fundamental right.

14. Danson v. Casey, 399 A.2d 360, 366 (Pa. 1979).

15. Thompson v. Engelking, 537 P.2d 635, 642 (Idaho, 1975).

16. Woodahl v. Straub, 520 P.2d 776, 782 (Mont. 1974), *cert. denied,* 419 U.S. 845 (1974).

17. Milliken v. Green, 203 N.W.2d 457 (Mich. 1972).

18. 212 N.W.2d 711 (Mich. 1973).

19. Thomas v. Stewart, No. 8275 (Ga. Super., Polk County, 1981), *rev'd. sub nom.* McDaniel v. Thomas, 285 S.E.2d 156 (Ga. 1981).

20. For a detailed discussion of the strict scrutiny equal protection test, see both the majority and dissenting opinions in Rodriguez, 411 U.S. 1 (1973). *See also,* Gerald Gunther, "The Supreme Court Foreward: In Search of Evolving Doctrine on a Changing Court: A Model for a Newer Equal Protection," *Harvard Law Review,* 86, no. 1 (1972):1.

21. Serrano v. Priest, 487 P.2d 1241 (Cal. 1971) (Serrano I); Serrano v. Priest, 557 P.2d 929 (Cal. 1976) (Serrano II). *See also* Caldwell v. Kansas, No. 50616 (D. Kan. 1972); Van Dusartz v. Hatfield, 334 F. Supp. 870 (D. Minn. 1971).

22. 557 P.2d 929, 948-52 (1976). See text with note 4 for a discussion of the *Rodriguez* decision.

23. *Id.* at 953.

24. *Id.* at 939.

25. 487 P.2d 1241, 1265 (1971); 557 P.2d 929, 947 (1976).

26. Horton v. Meskill, 332 A.2d 113 (Conn. 1974).

27. *Id.* at 118.

28. *Id.* at 117.

29. Washakie County School District No. 1 v. Herschler, 606 P.2d 310, 334 (Wyo. 1980), *cert. denied sub nom.* Hot Springs County School Dist. No. One v. Washakie County School Dist. No. 1, 449 U.S. 824 (1980).

30. Pauley v. Kelly, 255 S.E.2d 859, 878 (W. Va. 1979). *See* text with note 59 for a discussion of the court's interpretation of state constitutional mandates in this case.

31. Somerset County Bd. of Educ. v. Hornbeck (Md. Cir. Ct., Baltimore City, 1979), reported in *Education Daily,* 21 May 1981, pp. 1-2.

32. Alma School Dist. v. Dupree, No. 77-406 (Ark. Chancery, Pulaski County, 1981).

33. Lujan v. State Bd. of Educ., No. 79 SA 276 (D. Colo. 1979). Oral arguments were heard before the Colorado Supreme Court on 14 September 1981. *See also* Colorado Legislative Council, *Report to the Colorado General Assembly: Recommendations for 1980 Committee on School Finance* (Denver: State of Colorado, 1979), pp. 38-49.

34. Board of Educ., Levittown Union Free School Dist., Nassau County v. Nyquist, 408 N.Y.S.2d 606, 636 (Sup. Ct. Nassau County, 1978). The court cited Matter of Levy, 382 N.Y.S.2d 13 (N.Y. 1976), in which the New York high court had ruled that education is not such a fundamental state constitutional right as to invoke the strict scrutiny equal protection standard of review.

35. *Id.,* 408 N.Y.S. 2d 636. For a discussion of the middle-level, equal-protection test *see* Craig v. Boren, 429 U.S. 190, 197 (1976).

36. *Id.*, 408 N.Y.S.2d 644.

37. *Id.*, 443 N.Y.S.2d 843 (App. Div. 1981).

38. Equal protection analysis can focus on inputs, opportunities, or outcomes from several perspectives (e.g., students, taxpayers), but courts usually have focused on interdistrict resource disparities in equal protection challenges to state school finance schemes.

39. Robinson v. Cahill, 287 A.2d 187 (N.J. Super. 1972), *aff'd as modified*, 303 A.2d 273, 283-85 (N.J. 1973) (Robinson I).

40. *Id.* at 295.

41. *Id.* at 297-98.

42. *See* Robinson II, 306 A.2d 65 (N.J. 1973); Robinson III, 339 A.2d 193 (N.J. 1975); Robinson IV, 351 A.2d 713 (N.J. 1975); Robinson V, 355 A.2d 129 (N.J. 1976); Robinson VI, 358 A.2d 457 (N.J. 1976).

43. 351 A.2d 713, 719 (N.J. 1975).

44. *Id.* at 726 (Pashman, J., separate opinion).

45. *See* N.J.S.A. 18A:7A-1, *et seq.*

46. N.J.S.A. 18A:7A-5. *See* chapter 3, text with note 20, for a discussion of this law.

47. N.J.S.A. 18A:7A-14 and 7A-15.

48. 355 A.2d 129 (N.J. 1976).

49. 358 A.2d 457 (N.J. 1976). *See also In re* Board of Educ. of the City of Trenton, 424 A.2d 435 (N.J. 1980).

50. In fact, it has been reported that the New Jersey reform efforts have not resulted in as much equalization as had been expected, especially for urban school districts. *See* Fred Burke, *The Four Year Assessment of the Public School Education Act of 1975* (Trenton, N.J.: New Jersey State Board of Education, 1980), pp. 1, 4, and chapter 3; John Augenblick, *School Finance Reform in the States: 1979* (Denver, Colo.: Education Commission of the States 1979), p. 43. Recently, 20 students and the Newark Board of Education initiated a suit against the state, charging that the current school law is no more constitutional than the 1970 law invalidated in the original *Robinson* v. *Cahill* decision. *See Education Daily*, 10 December 1981, pp. 5-6.

51. Northshore School Dist. No. 417 v. Kinnear, 530 P.2d 178 (Wash. 1974).

52. *Id.* at 202.

53. Seattle School Dist. No. 1 of King County v. Washington, 585 P.2d 71 (Wash. 1978). In this case, the court overruled *Northshore*.

54. *Id.* at 102-4.

55. *Id.* at 96-97. The court disallowed reliance on special excess levies to fund the basic education program.

56. *Id.* at 95-96.

57. Pauley v. Kelly, 255 S.E.2d 859 (W. Va. 1979).

58. *Id.* at 878.

59. *Id.* at 865, n. 7.

60. *Id.* at 877.

61. *Id.* at 862.

62. *Id.* at 865, n. 7. In 1981 the West Virginia Supreme Court ruled that because of the "constitutionally preferred status of public education" the governor could not order a reduction in previously appropriated education funds (to avert a state deficit) without compelling factual justification. State *ex rel.* Board of Educ., County of Kanawha v. Rockefeller, nos. 15227, 15241 (W. Va. 1981). *See* Richard Meekley, "Court Grants Education a Preferred Funding Status in West Virginia," *Journal of Education Finance* 7, no. 2 (1981):227-29.

63. *Id.* at 878.

64. *See* Betsy Levin, "The Courts, Congress, and Educational Adequacy: The Equal Protection Predicament," *Maryland Law Review* 39 (1979): 254.

65. McInnis v. Shapiro, 293 F. Supp. 327, 335 (N.D. Ill. 1968), *aff'd mem. sub nom.* McInnis v. Ogilvie, 394 U.S. 322 (1969). *See also* Burruss v. Wilkerson, 310 F. Supp. 572 (W.D. Va. 1969), *aff'd. mem.*, 397 U.S. 44 (1970); Le Beauf v. State Bd. of Educ., 244 F. Supp. 256 (E.D. La. 1965).

66. 347 U.S. 483, 493 (1954).

67. *Brown* has been relied upon as precedent in challenges to alleged discrimination in connection with tracking schemes, testing procedures, and curricular offerings and in cases attacking the denial of school attendance to certain children. *See* Larry P. v. Riles, 495 F. Supp. 926 (N.D. Cal. 1979); Mills v. Board of Educ., 348 F. Supp. 866 (D.D.C. 1972); Hobson v. Hansen, 269 F. Supp. 401 (D.D.C. 1967); *aff'd sub nom.* Smuck v. Hobson, 408 F.2d 175 (D.C. Cir. 1969).

68. *See* Mills v. Board of Educ., *id.;* Pennsylvania Ass'n for Retarded Children v. Commonwealth, 343 F. Supp. 279 (E.D. Pa. 1972).

69. *See* Section 504 of the Rehabilitation Act, P.L. 93-112, 29 U.S.C. § 794 (1976); The Education for All Handicapped Children Act, P.L. 94-142, 20 U.S.C. § 1401 (1976); chapter 4, text with note 20.

70. *See* Mahoney v. Administrative School Dist. No. 1, 601 P.2d 826 (Ore. App. 1979); Doe v. Grile, 3 EHLR 551:285 (N.D. Ind. 1979); Lora v. Board of Education, 456 F. Supp. 1211 (E.D.N.Y. 1978); Frederick v. Thomas, 419 F. Supp. 960 (E.D. Pa. 1976), *aff'd,* 557 F.2d 373 (3d Cir. 1977), Mills v. Board of Educ., 348 F. Supp. 866 (D.D.C. 1972).

71. New York Ass'n for Retarded Children v. Carey, 466 F. Supp. 487 (E.D.N.Y. 1979).

72. In the Matter of Charles Hartman, 409 N.E.2d 1211 (Ind. App. 1980).

73. *See* Allan Odden and John Augenblick, *School Finance Reform in the States: 1980* (Denver, Colo.: Education Commission of the States, 1980), p. 5.

74. P.L. 88-352, 42 U.S.C. § 2000d-2000d-4 (1976). *See* chapter 4, text with note 6.

75. 414 U.S. 563 (1974).

76. Aspira v. Board of Educ. of the City of New York, No. 4002 (S.D.N.Y. 1974). *See also* Serna v. Portales Municipal Schools, 351 F. Supp. 1279 (D.N.M. 1972), *aff'd*, 499 F.2d 1147 (10th Cir. 1974).

77. United States v. State of Texas, 506 F. Supp. 405 (E.D. Tex. 1981). *See also* Idaho Migrant Council v. Board of Educ., 647 F.2d 69 (9th Cir. 1981).

78. *Id.*, 506 F. Supp. 437. The judge found the state's current plan to be inadequate in that bilingual instruction was required (and state supported) only in kindergarten through grade three where there were more than 20 English-deficient students in a grade. The order calls for bilingual instruction for *all* pupils having limited proficiency in English.

79. Guadalupe Org., Inc. v. Tempe Elementary School Dist. No. 3, 587 F.2d 1022 (9th Cir. 1978).

80. Keyes v. School Dist. No. 1, Denver Colorado, 521 F.2d 465 (10th Cir. 1975), *cert. denied*, 423 U.S. 1066 (1976).

81. Martin Luther King Elementary School Children v. Ann Arbor School Dist., 273 F. Supp. 1371 (E.D. Mich. 1979).

82. P.L. 93-380, 20 U.S.C. § 1701 (1976).

83. P.L. 94-142, 20 U.S.C. § 1401 *et seq.* (1976). *See* chapter 4, text with note 21, for a discussion of this law.

84. *See* Gary B. v. Cronin, 3 EHLR 551:633 (N.D. Ill. 1980); School Committee, Town of Truro v. Commonwealth of Massachusetts, 3 EHLR 552:186 (Mass. Super. 1980); North v. District of Columbia Bd. of Educ., 471 F. Supp. 136 (D.D.C. 1979); Matter of "A" Family, 606 P.2d 157 (Mont. 1979).

85. Tatro v. State of Texas, 481 F. Supp. 1224 (N. D. Tex. 1979), *vacated and remanded*, 625 F.2d 557 (5th Cir. 1980).

86. Armstrong v. Kline, 476 F. Supp. 583 (E.D. Pa. 1979), *aff'd* 629 F.2d 269 (3d Cir. 1980), *cert. denied sub nom.* Scanlon v. Battle, 101 S. Ct. 3123 (1981); (Georgia Ass'n of Retarded Citizens v. McDaniel, 511 F. Supp. 1263 (N.D. Ga. 1981); Mahoney v. Administrative School Dist. No. 1, 601 P.2d 826 (Ore. App. 1979).

87. Tatro v. State of Texas, 625 F.2d 557 (5th Cir. 1980).

88. *See Education Daily*, 21 January 1981, p. 3.

89. *See* Gladys J. v. Pearland Independent School District, 520 F. Supp. 869 (S.D. Tex.1981); Erdman v. Connecticut, 3 EHLR 552:218 (D. Conn. 1980); North v. District of Columbia Bd. of Educ., 471 F. Supp. 136 (D.D.C. 1979); Michael P. v. Maloney, 3 EHLR 551:155 (D. Conn. 1979); Grymes v. Madden, 3 EHLR 552:183 (D. Del. 1979); Matthews v. Campbell, 3 EHLR 551:265 (E.D. Va. 1979); Ladson v. Board of Educ., 3 EHLR 551:188 (D.D.C. 1979); In the Matter of Suzanne, 381 N.Y.S.2d 628 (Family Ct., Westchester County, 1976). However, school districts are not obligated to support such private placements, if initiated unilaterally by parents. *See*, for example, Stemple v. Board of Educ. of Prince George's County, 464 F. Supp. 258 (D. Md. 1979), *aff'd*, 623 F.2d 893 (4th Cir. 1980), *cert. denied*, 101 S. Ct. 1348 (1981); Lafko v. Wappingers Central School Dist., 427 N.Y.S.2d 529 (App. Div. 1980); Moran v. Board of Directors, School Dist. of Kansas City, 584 S.W.2d 154 (Mo. App. 1979); Lux v. Connecticut, 386 A.2d 644 (Conn. C.P. Fairfield County, 1977); *In re* Joseph, 366 N.Y.S.2d 259 (Family Ct., Queens County, 1975).

90. *See* Kruelle v. Biggs, 489 F. Supp. 169 (D. Del. 1980), *aff'd sub nom.* Kruelle v. New Castle County School Dist., 642 F.2d 687 (3d Cir. 1981); North v. District of Columbia Bd. of Educ., 471 F. Supp. 136 (D.D.C. 1979).

91. *See* Rowley v. Board of Educ. of the Hendrick Hudson School Dist., 483 F. Supp. 528 (S.D.N.Y. 1980); *aff'd*, 632 F.2d 945 (2d Cir. 1980); Hairston v. Drosick, 423 F. Supp. 180 (S.D. W. Va. 1976).

92. *See* Lora v. Board of Educ., 456 F. Supp. 1211 (E.D.N.Y. 1978); Frederick L. v. Thomas, 419 F. Supp. 960 (E.D. Pa. 1976).

93. Springdale School Dist. v. Grace, 494 F. Supp. 266 (W.D. Ark. 1980), *aff'd* 656 F.2d 300 (8th Cir. 1981).

94. Krawitz v. Commonwealth of Pennsylvania, 408 A.2d 1202 (Pa. Commw. 1979).

95. Armstrong v. Kline, 476 F. Supp. 583 (E.D. Pa. 1979).

96. Rowley v. Board of Educ. of the Hendrick Hudson School Dist., 483 F. Supp. 528 (S.D.N.Y. 1980).

97. Age v. Bullitt County Public Schools, 3 EHLR 551:505 (W.D. Ky. 1980). *See also* Kruelle v. Biggs, 489 F. Supp. 169 (D. Del. 1980); DeWalt v. Burkholder, 3 EHLR 551:550 (E.D. Va. 1980).

98. In the Matter of Charles Hartman, 409 N.E.2d 1211 (Ind. App. 1980).

99. *See Education Daily*, 18 July 1980, pp. 3-4.

100. Lora v. Board of Educ., 456 F. Supp. 1211, 1293 (E.D.N.Y. 1978).

101. Armstrong v. Kline, 476 F. Supp. 583 (E.D. Pa. 1979), *aff'd*, 629 F.2d 269 (3d Cir. 1980), *cert. denied sub nom.* Scanlon v. Battle, 101 S. Ct. 3123 (1981).

102. *See Education Daily*, 22 January 1981, p. 1.

103. 101 S. Ct. 3123 (1981).

104. Rowley v. Board of Educ. of the Hendrick Hudson School Dist., 483 F. Supp. 528 (S.D.N.Y. 1980), aff'd, 632 F.2d 945 (2d Cir. 1980).

105. See Education Daily, 14 January 1981, p. 4.

106. See Scoma v. The Chicago Bd. of Educ., 391 F. Supp. 452 (N.D. Ill. 1974); Board of Educ. of Aberdeen - Huntington Local School Dist. v. State Bd. of Educ., 189 N.E.2d 81 (Ohio App. 1962); Shoreline School Dist. v. Superior Court for King County, 346 P.2d 999, 1003 (Wash. 1959), cert. denied, 363 U.S. 814 (1960).

107. 406 U.S. 205 (1972).

108. Ed Nagel, "Home Schooling: The Epitome of Parental Involvement," Compact 14 (1979):31.

109. Education U.S.A. 22, no. 50 (11 August 1980):366.

110. State of Missouri v. Davis, 598 S.W.2d 189 (Mo. App. 1979).

111. State of West Virginia v. Riddle, 285 S.E.2d 359 (W. Va. 1981).

112. Id. at 366.

113. Id. at 364, citing Pauley v. Kelly, 255 S.E.2d 859 (1979). See text with note 60.

114. Pierce v. Society of Sisters, 268 U.S. 510 (1925).

115. See Wisconsin v. Yoder, 406 U.S. 205 (1972); Lemon v. Kurtzman, 403 U.S. 602 (1971); Board of Educ. v. Allen, 392 U.S. 236 (1968); Pierce v. Society of Sisters, 268 U.S. 510 (1925); Meyer v. Nebraska, 262 U.S. 390 (1923).

116. See Helen M. Jellison, State and Federal Laws Relating to Nonpublic Schools (Washington, D.C.: Department of Health, Education, and Welfare, 1975).

117. State ex rel. Nagel v. Olin, 415 N.E. 2d 281 (Ohio 1980); State of Ohio v. Whisner, 351 N.E.2d 750 (Ohio 1976).

118. Kentucky State Bd. for Elementary and Secondary Educ. v. Rudasill, 589 S.W.2d 877 (Ky. 1979), cert. denied, 446 U.S. 938 (1980). See Martha McCarthy, "Church and State: Separation or Accommodation?" Harvard Educational Review 51, no. 3 (1981):382.

119. State of North Dakota v. Shaver, 294 N.W.2d 883 (N.D. 1980).

120. State of Nebraska v. Faith Baptist Church, 301 N.W.2d 571, 579 (Neb. 1981), appeal dismissed, 102 S. Ct. 75 (1981).

121. Kentucky State Bd. for Elementary and Secondary Educ. v. Rudasill, 589 S.W.2d 877 (Ky. 1979), cert. denied, 446 U.S. 938 (1980).

122. See Brown v. Board of Educ., 347 U.S. 483 (1954); Larry P. v. Riles, 495 F. Supp. 926 (N.D. Cal. 1979); Hobson v. Hansen, 269 F. Supp. 401 (D.D.C. 1967), aff'd sub nom. Smuck v. Hobson, 408 F.2d 175 (D.C. Cir. 1969); Mills v. Board of

Educ., 348 F. Supp. 866 (D.D.C. 1972). Even though the federal judiciary has declined to scrutinize state school support schemes under equal protection guarantees, a few state courts have concluded that finance systems abridge the federal equal protection clause because they lack a rational relationship to a legitimate governmental goal. *See* text with notes 33 and 35.

123. Once a state establishes a property entitlement to certain services such as welfare benefits or education, it cannot take the entitlement away without providing due process of law. In Goss v. Lopez, 419 U.S. 565 (1975), the Supreme Court held that even a short-term suspension from school impaired a student's property right to an education. Challenges to state educational systems conceivably could allege that inadequacies in school offerings deprive students of their substantive due process right to an essential service (i.e., education) that has been assured by state law. Perhaps even resource inequities among districts could be challenged on substantive due process grounds since children with the same state entitlement to an education are actually receiving differential benefits depending on the school district of their residence. *See* Kern Alexander, "The Potential of Substantive Due Process for School Finance Litigation," *Journal of Education Finance* 6, no. 4 (1981):456-70.

124. 411 U.S. 1, 36 (1973). *See* text with note 4.

125. Several state courts have required legislatures to determine the components of a basic or adequate education. Other legislatures have done so without any specific judicial prodding. Some commentators believe that the legislative response provides the judicially manageable standards that courts previously found absent. *See* Levin, "The Courts, Congress, and Educational Adequacy: The Equal Protection Predicament," pp. 253-63. *See also* Pauley v. Kelly, 255 S.E.2d 859, 878-84 (W.Va. 1979).

126. Tyll van Geel, *Authority to Control the School Program* (Lexington, Mass.: D.C. Heath and Company, 1976), p. 42.

127. *See* Seattle School Dist. No. 1 of King County v. Washington, 585 P.2d 71, 95 (Wash. 1978).

# 3

# State Legislative and Regulatory Activity to Define and Establish Standards of Educational Adequacy

Traditionally, state educational laws have pertained primarily to school inputs and program specifications such as school funding, personnel certification, school facility requirements, compulsory attendance, textbook selection, health and safety standards, minimum course offerings, student transportation, and the school calendar.[1] Recently, however, there has been increasing legislative activity regarding school accountability, minimum student and teacher competencies, and the educational rights of handicapped and other special-need students. As states have assumed a greater share of the fiscal responsibility for education, legislative requirements for schools have increased.[2] In some states statutory directives are quite specific, whereas in others the state board of education and perhaps local school boards are delegated authority to develop specific standards for schools within broad legislative guidelines.

Despite the increase in state educational requirements, few state legislatures have attempted to define in a direct manner what an adequate education entails. Over half of the states participating in the recent federally funded studies of state school finance systems reported that there was no identifiable process for defining educational adequacy, and most of the remaining states indicated that adequacy was defined in terms of minimum school input specifications usually contained in state accreditation standards.[3] Thus the legislative posture regarding the essential features of an adequate education—one that is guaranteed to all children within the state—must be inferred from various legislative and administrative directives.

In this chapter we analyze state statutes and administrative regulations that directly or indirectly address educational adequacy concerns. The first section consists of an overview of features included in school funding laws. We then examine in some detail a few state statutes in which an attempt has been made to identify what constitutes an adequate education. The next three sections focus on state input and output specifications for schools (e.g., program requirements, student competencies), which serve as "proxies" for definitions of educational adequacy. In the final section we summarize the current legislative and regulatory activity, highlighting some of the problems associated with existing statutory and regulatory definitions and standards of educational adequacy.

## School Funding Laws in General

While most school finance laws do not define the elements of an adequate general education, inferences can be drawn from the features included in these funding statutes. Indeed, it might be argued that state aid allocation schemes reflect the *primary* legislative definition of educational adequacy; the components of an adequate education are those assured sufficient fiscal support. However, these laws usually earmark funds only for targeted pupil instructional programs and support services or for unique school district characteristics,[4] thereby offering little insight as to the legislature's posture on what comprises an adequate education for the normal-range student. One might contend that an adequate general education is being defined in part by a specified dollar figure (e.g., what $1,000 per pupil can purchase).

Various pupil weight factors are used in allocation schemes in several states, and these factors provide some insight as to legislative sentiments regarding the features of an adequate education. As of 1979, seven states reported that the allocation of general state aid was calculated on the basis of weighted pupils for specific programs. Eighteen other states reported the use of some pupil weightings to reflect such factors as grade levels, incidence of poverty, and broad program categories (e.g., special and vocational education).[5] By allocating funds on the basis of pupil characteristics and programmatic concerns, legislatures in these states have indicated that it costs more to provide an adequate education for some students than for others. In Florida, for example, the cost factor for a visually handicapped student is 3.56 compared to 1.0 for regular students in grades four through nine.[6]

However, there is considerable diversity among states in the way pupil weight factors are derived and used. Some pupil weights are calculated from a state average of expenses incurred in serving various types of students, others reflect costs associated with exemplary programs within the state, and still others are based on national research data pertaining to the costs of particular services and programs.[7] The use of such weighting systems implies that an adequate education must take into account varying pupil and program needs, but whether adequate programs are actually supported depends upon the accuracy of the weight factors employed.

All states make some provision in state aid formulas for targeted instructional programs, even if pupil weight factors are not used. Most of these targeted programs reflect federal educational priorities contained either in civil rights requirements or federal aid regulations. For example, funds are earmarked in every state for services and programs for children with physical and mental handicaps. Across all states, over $3.7 billion in state aid was being allocated for these special-need students in 1979.[8] State allocation formulas usually contain excess-cost reimbursement, categorical aid, extra classroom or teacher allotments, or weighted pupil categories for various types of handicapping conditions. These state aid provisions for the handicapped constitute the most explicit efforts to reflect in state school support systems the costs of providing adequate services and programs to meet particular student needs.

State allocation schemes usually target aid for specific programs in addition to those for the handicapped. Responding to provisions of the federal Vocational Education Act of 1963,[9] all states allocate funds for vocational education. Also, about half of the states either include pupil weight factors or categorical aid for compensatory education,[10] and 22 states make similar provisions for English-deficient students.[11] Several state allocation formulas also include weight factors or categorical aid for adult education, programs for gifted students, career education and occupational training, driver education, and preschool programs. Thus it can be inferred that through these provisions legislatures are defining, at least in part, the components of an adequate education.

Other features of school finance schemes that guarantee a minimum level of support for items such as textbooks, instructional materials, equipment, support personnel (e.g., counselors, psychologists, school nurses), transportation services, and school construction again reflect legislative thought as to the components of an adequate education. Many allocation formulas take into account teacher training and experience, and a few provide funding incentives to encourage additional formal education for instructional personnel.[12] Special weight factors for population sparsity and cost of living differentials among school districts (included in some state aid formulas) also suggest that an adequate educational program is considered more expensive to provide in some districts than in others.

Perhaps inferences for a definition of educational adequacy can even be drawn from the *absence* of certain features in allocation schemes. For example, aid usually is not tied to the attainment of specific pupil outcomes; thus most state support systems appear to reflect an input rather than an output orientation regarding the components of an adequate education.

# Statutory Definitions of an Adequate Education

As noted previously, only a few states have made *direct* attempts to define an adequate education through legislation. Some of the laws that do so have resulted from a judicial mandate for the legislature to define the components of the state-guaranteed educational program, while others have been enacted without external impetus. These statutes range in specificity, and the following are representative of legislative efforts in this area to date.[13]

## Arkansas

The Arkansas Quality of Education Act of 1969 defines educational adequacy primarily in terms of minimum school inputs.[14] It requires all elementary and secondary schools to submit to the state department of education an annual report upon which the school will be given an accreditation classification of "A," "B," or "C." Essentially, the statute prescribes school approval standards pertaining to personnel qualifications, course offerings, length of school term and instructional day, teaching loads and class size, graduation requirements, instructional materials, and financial support. Although not primarily a funding act, the law does empower the state board of education to provide supplemental funds for isolated schools or districts to assist them in complying with the standards. The law is unusual in that it statutorily prescribes specific school accreditation standards, rather than delegating the development of such requirements to the state board of education, as is true in most states. Moreover, the law imposes a sanction if one or more of a district's schools do not meet the standards for an "A" rating by a specified date or fall below an "A" rating for a period of more than two years. Such districts are to be annexed to the nearest district that is in compliance with the state requirements.

## Wisconsin

In 1973 Wisconsin enacted a school finance reform package, including state minimum standards of educational quality in addition to significant changes in the state aid scheme.[15] Among the purposes of the statute were to provide property tax relief, to promote greater equalization of expenditures among school districts, to limit spending increases through cost controls, and to guarantee basic educational opportunities for all students. To meet the objectives, the legislation provided for an increase in state-level funding, using revenue sources in addition to local property taxes. It also provided for equalization by guaranteeing a standard tax base for all districts. In fact, the act virtually eliminated—not merely minimized—the influence of a district's property tax base on educational spending by replacing the guaranteed minimum tax base with a standard base that substantially exceeded the state average equalized valuation. The law required districts with property valuation higher than the standard tax base to make payments to the state (negative aid).

The Wisconsin act stipulated that every school district meet 13 minimum standards in order to fulfill the state's obligation to provide all students with basic educational opportunities. The receipt of state aid was conditioned upon meeting these requirements. Three of the standards prescribed teacher qualifications, compensation, and inservice training. Another seven pertained to instructional offerings and services. The remaining standards concerned the provision of health services, safety of facilities, and required minimum levies for unconsolidated districts. Although the law has been amended because its negative aid provision was declared unconstitutional by the Wisconsin Supreme Court in 1976,[16] minimum program standards for schools have been retained as a condition of receiving state education funds.[17]

### Georgia

In 1974 the Georgia legislature enacted the Adequate Program for Education in Georgia Act, which is intended, in part, to assure "each Georgian an adequate educational opportunity to develop competencies necessary . . . to be effective workers and responsible citizens."[18] The statute requires the state board of education to establish minimum statewide standards and performance-based criteria to assure each child access to a quality program. The instructional program of each public school is to be evaluated on the basis of these standards and criteria. The law also requires the state board to make statewide assessments of school effectiveness at least once annually on a minimum of three grade levels. The state board is empowered to withhold state funds from any district failing to comply with the standards.

The statute provides for a foundation program with an unfunded district power equalizing formula. The foundation program covers 13 areas, and allotments are based on pupils in average daily attendance or instructional units. Included in the "calculated cost of instructional services" are items such as special education and preschool programs; instructional, administrative, supervisory, clerical, and student support personnel salaries and benefits; purchase and repair of instructional media and equipment; maintenance and operation expenses; pupil transportation; and expenses for isolated schools.[19] Each district is required to raise a percentage of the state's total required local effort (RLE) based on the district's portion of the state's property wealth. Local mill levies in excess of the RLE are unequalized. In addition to the foundation program, the law provides funds for capital facility improvements and prescribes procedures for facility inventories, surveys, and planning activities. The state board is empowered to establish priorities for capital outlay allotments.

While the intent of the Georgia law is to enhance equalization and to ensure each child an adequate educational opportunity, there are discrepancies between how the law is written and funded. The legislature recognized that the availability of funds would limit the law's implementation. In fact, the law empowers the state board to reduce allocations to local units if legislative appropriations are not sufficient to finance the state's portion of the foundation program. Thus the law does not guarantee adequate or equitable funding, although it purports to ensure an adequate education for all students within the state.

## New Jersey

In response to the *Robinson* v. *Cahill* litigation, the New Jersey legislature passed the Public School Education Act of 1975 to fulfill the state's obligation to support a thorough and efficient system of free public schools. The act specifies the following components of a thorough and efficient system:

1. Establishment of educational goals at both the state and local levels;

2. Encouragement of public involvement in the establishment of educational goals;

3. Instruction intended to produce the attainment of reasonable levels of proficiency in the basic communications and computational skills;

4. A breadth of program offerings designed to develop the individual talents and abilities of pupils;

5. Programs and supportive services for all pupils especially those who are educationally disadvantaged or who have special educational needs;

6. Adequately equipped, sanitary, and secure physical facilities and adequate materials and supplies;

7. Qualified instructional and other personnel;

8. Efficient administrative procedures;

9. An adequate state program of research and development; and

10. Evaluation and monitoring programs at both the state and local levels.[20]

The state board of education is required to establish a statewide pupil assessment program and specific statewide standards of pupil proficiency in basic communications and computational skills. These standards must be reasonably related to the levels of proficiency ultimately necessary for individuals to function politically, economically, and socially in a democratic society. Also, at least once every five years, the board is to direct and publicize the results of a comprehensive needs assessment of all the students in the state in light of the state's goals and standards. The act empowers the state commissioner of education to obtain a court order to force local district compliance with the state requirements. All districts are also required to specify *local* educational goals and standards, assess needs, develop programs to meet the needs, and evaluate the effectiveness of the programs. Local districts are encouraged to go beyond the state minimum basic skills requirements in their educational plans. Local initiative is further encouraged in that specific strategies to meet both state and local goals are left to local determination.

To accomplish greater equalization in school revenues and tax burden across districts, the act requires a significant increase in state level funding and a guaranteed tax yield. Local districts are allowed some flexibility in establishing tax rates, but caps are set on annual budget increases. However, districts can secure cap waivers, and surplus funds from the previous year are not included in the budget increase limitation.

## South Carolina

South Carolina enacted the Education Finance Act of 1977,[21] which establishes a pupil weighting classification scheme for the distribution of state educational aid, including incentives for strengthening the credentials of instructional personnel. In addition, the act requires the state board of education to develop a "defined minimum program" to be available to each child notwithstanding geographic differences and varying local economic factors. The act is intended to guarantee "to each student in the public schools of South Carolina the availability of at least minimum educational programs and services appropriate to his needs." The law stipulates that the base student cost is to be established annually by the legislature and is to approximate the cost of the defined minimum program as set forth by the state board of education. Most of the details of the program are left to the discretion of the state board; however, the act does require specific teacher/pupil ratios, a state minimum salary schedule, annual school district reports on programmatic needs in light of the defined minimum program, and state board review of the defined minimum program.

## Washington

As a result of the *Seattle* case,[22] Washington's Basic Education Act was amended in 1979[23] and represents one of the most explicit legislative attempts to define the components of a basic or adequate education that must be provided to all students within the state. The law mandates that specific percentages of the total instructional program must be devoted to basic skill and work skill instruction. Basic skill areas are defined as reading/language arts (which may include foreign languages), mathematics, social sciences, science, music, art, health, and physical education. Work skill areas include industrial arts, home and family life education, business and office education, vocational education, trade and industrial education, technical education, and career education. Only 5% of the total instructional program is left for local district determination. In delineating the components of the basic education program, the legislature drew upon past practices within the state. Essentially, the content of the required program reflects the norm already in operation as to the types of programs offered in kindergarten through grade twelve. The state board of education is required to establish rules to implement the basic program and to ensure compliance throughout the state.

To assure full support of the basic program, the act replaces Washington's minimum foundation program with a funding scheme based on staff units. Staff units are allocated on the basis of student population, with modifications for factors such as population sparsity and declining enrollment. Additional staff units are provided for support services, and state categorical programs continue to fund special education, compensatory instruction, and other targeted programs. Local districts may supplement the basic education program up to 10% of the previous year's level of funding. Since the state funding formula is part of the Basic Education Act, it is not subject to legislative budget revisions unless the act itself is amended.

### Virginia

Virginia is unique in that its statutory provisions pertaining to educational adequacy emanate from a state constitutional mandate for the state board of education to prescribe educational "standards of quality," subject to revision only by the Virginia General Assembly.[24] The board develops these standards every two years and presents them to the legislature for review and approval. The statute specifies that all schools must comply with the standards pertaining to curriculum, finance, transportation, special education, facilities, textbooks, personnel qualifications, and other areas determined by the state board. The law requires each school district to develop an annual plan to meet the standards; a state-appointed team is to assess the plan's implementation. Each district also is required to involve staff and the community in revising and extending biennially a six-year improvement plan that is submitted to the state board of education for approval. Virginia's state formula for funding schools is based on a guaranteed level of support per pupil to implement these standards. However, the actual per pupil dollar amount, determined annually by the legislature, may or may not represent the actual costs associated with implementing the standards. Thus school districts are required to comply with the standards regardless of whether sufficient state aid is provided.[25]

## West Virginia

Partially in response to recent litigation, the West Virginia legislature extensively revised its school funding statute in 1981.[26] The amended law provides state aid for local districts to implement instructional improvement plans, revises property assessment practices, creates a new division of facilities planning and evaluation, revises the state minimum salary schedule and minimum teacher/pupil ratio, and requires the state board of education to develop standards of quality that must be satisfied by all school districts.

Like Virginia, the West Virginia Board of Education is charged with developing quality standards pertaining to curriculum, transportation, special education, facilities, textbooks, personnel qualifications, and any other areas determined by the state board. Local districts are allowed some flexibility in developing school improvement programs to address local needs as long as the minimum state standards are met. On-site review by the state board is required every fourth year to assess whether the state standards are being satisfied. Three types of status have been designated: 1) full approval, 2) probationary, and 3) nonapproval. Districts given probationary or nonapproval status lose part of their state aid.

State education aid is not directly tied to the newly required standards of quality in West Virginia, even though there is a financial penalty for noncompliance. However, the foundation program does assure support for certain program components such as specified pupil/teacher ratio, a minimum personnel salary schedule, and transportation costs. The funding formula also provides incentives for staff improvement and bases allocations for capital expenditures on district needs.

## Summary of State Laws

The laws discussed above represent a range in specificity and in approaches to defining educational adequacy. Essentially, the Arkansas, Wisconsin, Virginia, and Washington statutes prescribe school approval standards that pertain mainly to resource inputs and program specifications; thus they are similar to accreditation criteria devised by state boards of education in many other states. The Georgia, South Carolina, New Jersey, and West Virginia statutes, on the other hand, do not contain specific school standards. They explicate statewide educational goals, but delegate to the state board of education the responsibility to establish specific requirements that all schools must satisfy. The definition of educational adequacy contained in most of these statutes focuses on the school's responsibility to ensure that an adequate *program* is made available to all students. In addition to reflecting this concern, the Georgia and New Jersey laws also emphasize the school's responsibility to produce certain *outcomes* in terms of pupil achievement.

While these states have made an attempt to explicate what an adequate education entails, such specifications are reflected in varying degrees in the state school support schemes. For example, some provisions of the Georgia law have never been funded. Both the Virginia and South Carolina statutes stipulate that the state must ensure support of an educational program throughout the state that satisfies standards prescribed by the state board, but annual legislative appropriations have not always matched the state education department's cost figures for implementing the standards. Only the Washington law *directly* ties state aid to the *statutory* definition of an adequate basic education program and assures full state support of the program. But even in this state the actual adequacy of the guaranteed program has not been substantiated. The Washington law has had an equalizing effect in that all school districts have been assured full funding of the basic education program. Yet the components of this program have been determined by existing practices rather than by data relating program features to the attainment of specific educational goals. Conceivably, the state could decide to eliminate kindergarten or even an aspect of basic skill instruction from the required program. Since full state funding of educational expenditures other than the basic program is not guaranteed, identification of this program's components is of paramount importance.

## Program Requirements

In most states, educational adequacy is gauged primarily by state-imposed program specifications. All states by law require certain subjects (e.g., American history, English, physical education) to be taught in public schools. Connecticut's statutory course prescriptions are typical:

> In the public schools the program of instruction offered shall include at least the following subject matter, as taught by legally qualified teachers: the arts; career education; consumer education; health and safety; language arts, including reading, writing, grammar, speaking and spelling; mathematics; physical education; science; social studies, including, but not limited to citizenship, economics, geography, government and history; and in addition,

on at least the secondary level, one or more foreign languages and vocational education.[27]

Although some states legislatively stipulate specific teacher/pupil ratios, personnel qualifications, graduation requirements, etc., usually state boards of education are authorized to develop specific criteria that schools must satisfy. In about half of the states, local boards of education are empowered to adopt courses of study, but generally they must secure state board approval.[28] Thus, the standards promulgated by state boards of education represent the most explicit data source currently available regarding how states define an adequate education in terms of program requirements.

The bulk of these program specifications are contained in state accreditation or school approval schemes. Many states have modeled such schemes on standards and procedures used by private accrediting agencies—the pioneers in establishing input criteria to evaluate the adequacy of schools.[29] Indeed, most state requirements closely parallel or actually incorporate the resource and program standards of the state's respective private regional association. These association standards usually are devised by a task force of educational professionals, with advice from member schools. To receive accreditation from a regional association, schools are required to conduct a comprehensive self-study that includes developing a plan to correct deficiencies noted. While regional accreditation standards are flexible to provide for variations among schools in purposes and programs, such variations are expected to exist within a "common framework of preconditions" for quality education.[30]

Most state school-approval schemes, like those of the private associations, focus primarily on program inputs (e.g., teacher qualifications, course offerings, instructional time, materials, teacher/pupil ratio, facilities). In some states public schools are required to provide remedial programs for students with identified deficiencies, but in no state is school approval based on the attainment of outcomes (e.g., student mastery of minimum competencies).

States differ as to the level of specificity included in state accreditation criteria. In some states the criteria include precise specifications for instructional facilities to be provided (e.g., art room, music room, gymnasium, science labs, etc.) and prescribe the minimum amount of instructional time in each area of the curriculum. For example, Indiana's accreditation standards for elementary schools include specific time allocations for kindergarten instruction pertaining to language experiences (50%), creative experiences (15%), personal growth experiences (10%), social living and environmental experiences (15%), and mathematical experiences (10%).[31] In contrast, some state standards are couched in general terms and do not include specific criteria for making an assessment of whether the standard has been satisfied. For example, a standard for kindergartens in Kentucky prescribes that the "program shall include desirable experiences in social living, physical development, emotional growth and stability, language arts, science, music, art, and creative activities . . . in accordance with each child's level of comprehension and maturation."[32] The standard does not define the terms or specify criteria for judging compliance. The most comprehensive state-level standards are found in states with a history of a high level of state support, particularly those in the Southeast.[33] In a few states local districts retain considerable discretion in establishing criteria for assessing educational adequacy.

In approximately half of the states, procedures have been adopted in which school districts engage in a process of evaluating their own educational programs with technical assistance provided by state education department personnel.[34] In some states school districts must engage in this self-evaluation process as a condition of receiving state aid, whereas in others participation is voluntary. In still other instances school districts are required to satisfy minimum state standards and are provided the option of engaging in a self-evaluation process. In these self-assessments school districts are required to identify their needs, design goals and objectives, develop strategies to meet the objectives, and devise evaluation systems. Thus standards by which adequacy is judged may vary among school districts according to locally identified needs and goals.

Some states classify districts according to their compliance with school approval or accreditation standards and condition state education aid on compliance with minimum state standards.[35] In Texas, for example, all school districts must satisfy detailed state requirements ("Principles and Standards") and develop a five-year plan for improvement in order to qualify for state financial support.[36] Similarly, all Colorado school districts must receive "standard accreditation," which signifies that the district satisfies minimum criteria adopted by the state board of education. In addition, Colorado districts can participate in the optional "Accreditation by Contract" program in which the district makes a commitment to implement a comprehensive and continuous school improvement plan. Participating districts make a contract with the state board of education to identify goals and objectives and strategies to attain them.[37]

The use of self-evaluations in accreditation programs has considerable appeal because it allows for differences among local districts as to specific educational objectives and strategies to attain them. Indeed, if educational adequacy were gauged entirely by such self-studies, one would expect standards of adequacy to vary considerably throughout a state, based on locally identified needs and priorities. Carrying this strategy to its logical conclusion, the distribution of state educational funds would reflect such variations among school districts.

## Accountability Mandates

While state accreditation and approval schemes usually focus on ensuring that all schools satisfy minimum standards pertaining to specific resource inputs and programmatic features, they are based on the assumption that compliance with such requirements will have a positive effect on school outcomes, primarily student achievement. However, the assumption that fulfillment of certain input criteria will produce the desired outcomes has been seriously questioned in recent years. Public demands for accountability have accelerated because of dissatisfaction with pupil academic achievement and teacher effectiveness. Inflation, rising taxes, and the general feeling that the public is not receiving a good return for its financial investment in education have given rise to legislation designed to improve the efficiency of the educational enterprise and to render schools accountable to the public that supports them.

This accountability legislation has proliferated during the past two decades. Often, in their efforts to improve school productivity, legislators have borrowed systems approaches from military, industrial, and commercial institutions. Actually, the application of technical-industrial principles to education is not a new phenomenon. The accountability movement, which began in the latter 1960s resembles the early twentieth century scientific management movement. In both periods there was a climate of school criticism, economic pressure, and the notion that improved "efficiency" might be a panacea for all ills.[38]

Between 1963 and 1974, 30 states enacted legislation pertaining to educational accountability, and over a third of these states enacted more than one law.[39] By the latter 1970s, almost all of the states had mandated by legislation or administrative regulation that public schools engage in some type of process to ensure accountability for results.

While the term *accountability* is subject to multiple definitions and interpretations, it generally connotes a regulatory process that includes the identification of goals, assessment of the existing situation and the desired state, evaluation of alternative strategies to move toward the desired state, selection and implementation of a strategy, evaluation of results, and initiation of corrective measures.[40] Accountability connotes a formal assignment of responsibilities within the process and checks to ensure that such responsibilities are carried out. It calls for an assessment of each individual's impact on process and output so that accountability can be assigned to appropriate persons or groups within the system.[41] Some accountability models emphasize the provision of evaluative data on the system's operation, whereas others focus on the prescription of corrective measures once deficiencies are identified.

Educational accountability programs established during the 1960s were primarily state needs assessments (funded in part under ESEA Title III[42]) that were designed to identify priority educational needs within the state. Such efforts have been expanded to focus on the evaluation of programs, schools, and school districts, often using data from statewide student testing programs.[43] In addition, there has been a recent increase in legislative activity regarding teacher competency and personnel evaluation programs. Also, the application of modern management techniques to schools has resulted from demands for fiscal accountability. Among the most popular management strategies have been Planning, Programming, Budgeting Systems (PPBS); Management by Objectives (MBO); Management Information Systems (MIS); and Planning, Evaluation, Review Techniques (PERT).[44]

Most educational accountability mandates have been designed to improve the school's product in terms of pupil performance. Thus they have been grounded in the notion that an adequate education is one that produces specified results in terms of student achievement and produces such results in an efficient manner. Colorado's Educational Accountability Act of 1971, for example, calls for an assessment of "whether decisions affecting the educational process are advancing or impeding student achievement."[45] School accountability schemes usually have relied on the following assumptions underlying the technical-industrial accountability model:

1. There is a consensus as to desired outcomes of production.

2. There are measures for objective assessment of progress toward production goals.

3. There is a knowledge base that specifies the mode of production.

4. The production process can be controlled so that outside influences on production are minimized.

5. There is an incentive structure that motivates both labor and management to strive for efficiency in the production process.[46]

Attempts to apply the technical-industrial model to education have resulted in considerable frustration, because of the inherent differences between public education and business or industry. Some critics of school accountability efforts have argued that none of the above assumptions hold up in education,[47] and even proponents of such efforts agree that the educational system does not control one of the key parts of the regulatory process, i.e., the establishment of educational goals. Consensus does not exist on what should be the outcomes of schooling. Goals are often ill-defined or stated in such all-encompassing terms that operational objectives cannot be developed. It seems ironic that accountability schemes have been hailed as the means to ensure that the educational system fulfill goals that have not been articulated clearly. H. T. James observed in 1971 that "we have been notably unsuccessful as a society in this century in stating our aims of education."[48] Henry Dyer similarly noted that instead of concrete goals for schools, we have vague generalities:

> Educational goals, as commonly formulated by educational philosophers, have tended to be cast in such sweeping generalities and remote ideals that they have left school people at a loss to use them meaningfully for assessing the actual ongoing operations of their institutions. . . . The educational oratory speaks of goals like "self-fulfillment," "responsible citizenship," and "vocational effectiveness"; the assessment of school efficiency in specific cases usually depends on such measures as retention rate, average daily attendance, and performance on reading tests. Whether there are any rational connections between the numbers and the slogans is a matter that is rarely considered. The assumption seems to be implicit, for instance, that the longer a youngster stays in school, the greater will be his chances of self-fulfillment; or that the higher his reading score, the more likely he will become a responsible citizen. But such assumptions are left largely unexamined, and in particular cases may be obviously wrong.[49]

Lacking data substantiating what specific knowledge, skills, and behaviors are needed for various adult roles, school accountability efforts usually have focused on limited school outputs that are generally believed to be prerequisites to future success in life. Since there is widespread agreement that schools should teach students to read and compute, most measures of student outcomes included in accountability mandates have been restricted to student achievement in these narrow areas.[50] Tests traditionally employed have been norm-referenced, measuring student performance against a sample of peers. However, because of dissatisfaction with such instruments, many states have designed student assessment programs using criterion-referenced tests that measure performance against a predetermined standard of proficiency. In some instances the criterion-referenced tests are constructed at the state level on the basis of state-prescribed performance objectives,[51] while in other instances local school districts are charged with developing the tests on the basis of local objectives for student performance.

Several states are currently using testing materials and procedures developed by the National Assessment of Educational Progress (NAEP), which was established in 1969 through a contractual arrangement between the federal government and the Education Commission of the States.[52] Student achievement data are gathered by NAEP from a national sample of students at regular intervals. Performance objectives, with multiple test items for each objective, have been designed in 10 content areas, and over 1,700 test items keyed to these objectives have been made available for public use. Thus a state or local school district can select NAEP objectives and test items that match the instructional emphasis in the specific locale. A number of states, among them Arkansas, Connecticut, Maine, Massachusetts, and Minnesota, have conducted one or more statewide assessments following NAEP procedures. Such test results have been used in Maine to devise educational program improvements, to determine funding priorities, and to obtain federal grants for remedial programs.[53] In the early 1970s Minnesota pioneered in adapting NAEP materials for a state testing program in which some test items were used statewide while others were chosen according to each local district's instructional objectives.[54]

In many states testing programs have been developed without specific reliance on NAEP materials. Michigan's student assessment program exemplifies a program that is part of a comprehensive educational planning model. Criterion-referenced tests that relate to multiple state goals and objectives are used. The assessment program, adopted in 1970, constitutes one phase of the state educational evaluation process. Unlike many state accountability provisions, the Michigan legislation provides for the reallocation of educational funds to provide remedial assistance for students identified as having the greatest educational deficiencies in basic skills.[55]

Florida's Educational Accountability Act of 1971 also includes a pupil testing program as part of a comprehensive educational accountability system. Each year specific statewide educational objectives must be established for each grade level and subject.[56] The law calls for the use of criterion-referenced and norm-referenced tests to assess pupil progress and the degree of mastery of the specified educational objectives. School districts are required to furnish annual reports, and the reports are to be made public. Subsequent Florida legislation has prescribed a comprehensive management information and assessment system, including standardized reporting procedures and cost accounting and reporting on a school-by-school and district aggregate basis.[57]

Even though these accountability mandates (with their emphasis on the assessment of student performance in academic skills) are intended to supply data so that schools can be made more effective in terms of results, the data gathered usually are not used to make changes in school support systems. The translation of student achievement data into resource allocation is problematic, given current educational technology. Data relating student performance to particular pedagogical procedures are insufficient,[58] and much of the research on the effectiveness of instructional materials consists of formal or informal market research.[59] Possibly, the attention directed toward educational outcomes through accountability mandates ultimately will result in more systematic efforts to document the determinants of those outcomes.

Accountability mandates also may bring into sharper focus the need to formulate concrete goals for public education that can be converted into measures of school productivity. The current discrepancies between program specifications for schools (which include areas such as career education,[60] physical education, and the creative arts) and measures used to assess school effectiveness (which are primarily confined to student achievement in basic skills) might be resolved by refocusing both program requirements and outcome measures in light of clearly defined goals and objectives.

## Minimum Student Competencies

Partly because of the ambiguity as to the desired outcomes of schooling, there has been substantial recent activity to explicate minimum competencies that should be acquired by all students. These efforts represent the most direct attempt to define educational adequacy in terms of student outcomes; that is, an adequate education assures student acquisition of a prespecified set of competencies. Some minimum competency programs are prescribed as part of comprehensive educational accountability systems.

By 1976 only four states had enacted student competency legislation, but three years later 36 states had either laws or administrative regulations requiring students to exhibit certain competencies as a prerequisite to high school graduation or promotion from one grade to the next.[61] Since all remaining states have studies or proposals underway regarding minimum student competencies, it cannot be denied that minimum competency testing (MCT) has become a pervasive and controversial national movement.

In a 1978 survey of the 50 states, *Today's Education* defined MCT as "any program of assessment, evaluation, certification, or testing (not necessarily paper and pencil) that is designed to determine whether individual students have reached a minimum level of performance predetermined as satisfactory."[62] While the focus of MCT programs is on the individual learner, an underlying assumption is that such programs will make school districts more accountable for teaching the required skills. Notable state programs include Oregon's Goal Based Program, Florida's Functional Literacy Skills Program, New York's Pupil Evaluation Program, and Maryland's Alternative Accountability Pilot Project.[63] There even has been a movement to establish national standards, exemplified by the Mottl Bill, introduced in Congress in 1977, which would have established a national commission on basic education to develop reading, writing, and arithmetic skills tests for specified grades.[64]

In some states competency standards are mandated at the state level, while in others standards are devised locally. There is also diversity in how competency tests are used. In 18 states students must pass competency examinations as a prerequisite to graduation from high school.[65] In other states local school boards have the option of determining how to evaluate competencies and use these data, or MCT is used solely to identify remediation needs among students. In 13 states the MCT program requires remediation efforts for students identified as deficient in basic skill areas.[66]

The Education Commission of the States reported in 1978 that all but one of the states using MCT as part of minimum requirements for high school graduation included measures of competence in reading, writing, and arithmetic, and over half focused solely on this triad. Only a few states reported that MCT programs addressed consumerism, problem-solving ability, and other areas that might be classified as life skills.[67] Thus it appears that MCT programs primarily have been restricted to an assessment of student performance in the basic academic skills. Possibly this focus exists because of consensus that academic skills are the most important in assuring future success in life, but more likely the emphasis has been due to the fact that these skills are the easiest to assess with the current level of psychometric sophistication.[68]

The cost/benefit aspect of student minimum competency requirements has been the source of continual debate. Anderson reported in 1977 that the total costs of mandated minimum competency programs can be overwhelming, even when the added expenditures for remediation programs are not included.[69] He found that there are hidden costs associated with state regulatory efforts as well as direct costs for test development, test administration, development and maintenance of monitoring mechanisms, and add-on costs for compensatory education programs. Critics of MCT programs have contended that the redistribution of school resources to meet testing and remediation expenses might result in a narrowing of the curriculum and the possible elimination of experiences to nurture creative expression.[70] Concern has also been voiced that the focus on "minimums" may be destructive of the principle of intellectual and personal meritocracy in education.[71]

However, advocates of MCT programs have countered these assertions by arguing that the curriculum possibly needs to be more limited and clearly focused to assure that minimum competencies in basic skill areas are being mastered by students.[72] Publicity pertaining to the high percentage of students who have failed minimum competency examinations has provided support for the contention that schools have been promoting and even graduating students who have not mastered essential basic skills. For example, it was reported in 1981 that 6,000 Washington, D.C. students in grades one through three failed competency tests in both reading and math skills, and over half of the district's primary school students failed at least one of the tests.[73] It has been asserted that with MCT programs such deficiencies can be identified early in a child's schooling so that remediation can be provided.[74] It has also been claimed that MCT programs can increase school effectiveness by ensuring better articulation between the curriculum and student assessment.[75]

The minimum competency programs in two states are described briefly below as illustrations of efforts to define educational adequacy from the standpoint of minimum student competencies. Oregon represents a decentralized minimum competency program and Florida provides a highly centralized approach. These states were selected because Oregon pioneered in the minimum competency movement, and Florida has implemented the most comprehensive MCT program to date.

### Student Competencies: Oregon

Oregon was one of the first states to make a systematic effort to adopt state standards pertaining to student competencies extending beyond academic performance in basic skills. Concern for student outcomes was evident in the statewide goals adopted by the Oregon Board of Education in 1974. The goals stipulated that "each individual will have the opportunity to develop to the best of his or her ability the knowledge, skills, and attitudes necessary to function effectively in six life roles: the individual, the learner, the producer, the citizen, the consumer, and the family member."[76] The state educational standards reinforced this life-role concept in that each school's curriculum—including planning and evaluation results—was required to be compatible with the statewide goals. Furthermore, in accordance with the goals, students were required to demonstrate competence in ten areas as well as to satisfy course requirements as a prerequisite for a high school diploma.

When the state board introduced the minimum competencies requirement, the intent was to provide a means to assure that Oregon's high school graduates would be able to cope adequately with the demands commonly faced in adulthood. The state board delegated the authority and responsibility for developing specific competencies to the local school boards, believing that competencies should reflect the cultural and societal goals of the local community. Such competency lists were to be limited to those that the local board of education could support as acceptable evidence that its schools had provided students with the basic minimum abilities needed to function in the six life roles identified above. Also, local districts were given a great deal of freedom to determine *how* they would meet the competency standards. For example, districts could allow students to earn credits and/or demonstrate minimum competencies through community service, independent study, and work experience. Districts also could choose means of assessing student competency, which might include teacher testimonials and course completion as well as written examinations.[77]

Thus a school district, although required to attest to the fact that certain competencies have been mastered by students, might use means for making that determination that traditionally have been used in assessing student performance. The major difference is that with the minimum competency requirement the school board must verify not only that certain courses have been completed but also that specific competencies have been acquired. Oregon, therefore, may have strengthened the grounds for students to assert instructional negligence. If a student can produce evidence that a given competency actually has not been mastered, although documented as having been, a court might conclude that school authorities have been negligent in carrying out their charge from the state.[78]

Since Oregon school districts also have latitude in deciding *what* competencies must be mastered, proficiency standards for high school graduation differ widely throughout the state. Thus, student transfers pose a serious problem, and data on student competencies cannot be aggregated across districts. These concerns could be alleviated by using a uniform set of competencies and assessment strategies statewide. However, the latter course would threaten local decision-making prerogatives by shifting curriculum decisions to the state level. While Oregon policy makers have opted for local control in establishing student competency standards, the educational and political implications of state versus local development of minimum competency programs are generating substantial controversy in many other states.

### Student Competencies: Florida

Florida's program has perhaps received the most national attention among MCT efforts. Florida's commitment to educational accountability started in the 1960s and culminated in the Educational Accountability Act of 1976 that prescribed minimum graduation standards for students graduating from high school after 1979. Among the purposes of the act were to:

1. Provide a system of accountability for education in Florida which guarantees that each student is afforded similar opportunities for educa-

tional advancement without regard to geographic differences and varying local economic factors;

2. Guarantee to each student in the Florida system of public education that the system provides instructional programs which meet minimum performance standards compatible with the state's plan for education; and

3. Provide information to the public about the performance of the Florida system of public education in meeting established goals and providing effective, meaningful, and relevant educational experiences designed to give students at least the minimum skills necessary to function and survive in today's society.[79]

The act includes statewide testing and assessment components as well as provisions for district assessment programs. The major outcomes of the act have been the development of the Basic Skills Test and the Functional Literacy Test. The Basic Skills Test measures appropriate skills agreed upon by educators as minimal for grades three, five, and eight. Functional literacy has been defined by the Florida Department of Education as the ability to apply the basic skills in reading, writing, and mathematics to problems and tasks of a practical nature or to problems encountered in everyday life.[80] The Functional Literacy Test covers 24 skills in communications and mathematics. This test differs from the basic skills test in that it presents practical applications of selected academic skills. For example, in the communication section students are asked to use highway and city maps, use an index to locate information, distinguish between fact and opinion, and determine the cause and effect of an action.

Passage of the Functional Literacy Test as a prerequisite to high school graduation has been legally challenged. Plaintiffs charged that the test discriminated against students on the basis of race and ethnic background, included items that had not been taught in Florida schools, and was implemented without adequate notice to students. In 1981 the Fifth Circuit Court of Appeals upheld the use of the test for remediation purposes but enjoined its use as a prerequisite for a high school diploma.[81] The appeals court concluded that such a test could not be used as a graduation requirement without proof of its curricular validity. In other words, the state must establish that the Functional Literacy Test covers what actually has been taught in Florida schools. Furthermore, the court held that such a test (assuming its validity) could not be used as a diploma sanction until the 1982-83 school year to provide sufficient time to eliminate the effects of a past racial discrimination in the state. The court noted that the immediate use of such a test would be unfair to minority students, whose deficiencies have resulted in part from the prevalent school segregation in Florida prior to

1971. The waiting period was also considered necessary to provide students adequate notice regarding the skills covered on the tests.

Both the Oregon and Florida experiences in implementing MCT programs highlight many unresolved issues. What are the skills necessary for success in various life roles? How should competence be assessed? Should competencies be identified at the state or local levels? How "minimum" should the competencies be? What should be done with students who do not demonstrate proficiency? How should competency standards be reflected in the allocation of resources?

If an adequate education ultimately is to be defined as one that assures student mastery of minimum competencies, substantial research will be required for such a definition to be translated into state school support schemes. Currently, cost data that relate specific competencies to program features and resource inputs are not available. While numerous states are mandating that minimum student competencies be defined and assessed and that deficient students be provided remediation, the costs of these activities usually are not reflected in state aid formulas.

## Summary and Implications of Statutory and Regulatory Activity

Only a few states have attempted to identify by statute the specific components of an adequate education. Even these few attempts have been primarily input-oriented, with little documentation of the relationship between the prescribed programmatic features and educational goals that are generally couched in global terms. Instead of defining educational adequacy by statute, most legislatures have delegated to state boards of education the authority to prescribe specific standards that schools must satisfy.

Accordingly, state boards have promulgated numerous educational regulations, the majority of which are designed by state department personnel and pertain to minimum input specifications. These requirements serve as "proxies" for a definition of educational adequacy in most states. For example, if state regulations require specific course offerings, a school's program is considered inadequate if it fails to include such courses. Many of these standards are reflected in state school accreditation or approval schemes, but others are promulgated independently of accreditation activities.

While these input standards are purported to be grounded in a firm knowledge base, substantiating their relationship to pupil performance, less than one percent of educational funds is earmarked for research activities in this arena.[82] Mandated pupil/teacher ratios provide an example of an input requirement that is based on inconclusive data as to the effects of class size on pupil achievement.[83] Input standards in some instances have been derived from the existing norm among schools within a state. Also, through lobbying efforts child advocacy groups and teacher organizations have been influential in determining school input requirements. A program conceivably could be considered adequate under an input-oriented definition, even though the skills the program is designed to impart have not been acquired by students.

The use of output instead of input definitions of educational adequacy appears more defensible, but this approach as currently used does not offer a panacea. Without clearly stated goals for public education, the desired outcomes of schooling remain ill-defined. In many instances the goals ascribed to schools are all-encompassing, reaching far beyond resource capabilities and the sophistication of educational technology. Moreover, attempts to assess whether schools are actually attaining these goals have been confined mainly to measures of pupil academic achievement in a few skill areas that lend themselves to group-administered testing procedures. Thus the measures used to assess the school's performance do not reflect the goals ascribed to education or the focus of a substantial part of the instructional program (e.g., physical education, the creative arts, etc.).

In an attempt to reduce this discrepancy, efforts have escalated to identify specific competencies that should be mastered by students. Yet, again, the success of such efforts has been impeded by political problems (e.g., How should the competencies be identified and by whom?) and technical problems (e.g., How should the competencies be assessed?). Current competency testing programs are vulnerable to legal challenge because of insufficient data substantiating that the tests are bias-free and valid measures of what actually has been taught. Moreover, there are no assurances that the competencies being assessed are the only (or most important) skills necessary to ensure success in the various adult roles for which they are purported to be prerequisites.

In many states there is little apparent coordination among efforts to design resource and program input specifications for schools and efforts to establish standards for pupil performance or to assess the effectiveness of schools. Statewide student testing programs often are operated independently of school approval or accreditation activities. In some situations student performance standards seem to bear little relationship to adopted program requirements, or perhaps they even reflect different notions as to the school's purpose. While a few states are attempting to address these inconsistencies through accountability mandates that include input, output, and process standards as part of a unified educational planning and evaluation model, the incongruities between means and ends have not been resolved.

One unanticipated result of the proliferation of state regulations, specifying what schools must provide and produce, may be an increase in educational malpractice litigation. To date, claims that school districts are legally responsible to ensure a specified level of student achievement have not prevailed.[84] But such allegations seem destined to continue. As legislatures and administrative agencies become more specific in delineating the outcomes that can be expected from public education and the components of guaranteed educational programs, future plaintiffs may be more successful in substantiating negligence charges. Conceivably, courts may award damages if state-required programs are not provided, if state-mandated skills are not acquired (although reported to have been), or if the skills taught do not adequately prepare students for adult roles.[85]

There are obvious risks associated with explicating the components of an adequate education—one that must be provided to all students in the state—especially if such mandates promise more than can be delivered, given the available resources and technology. Efforts to identify output measures of educational adequacy and reflect them in program and resource specifications face substantial barriers, not the least of which is delineation of concrete goals for public schools. Yet it must be kept in mind that attempts to define and assess educational adequacy are in their infancy and are experiencing predictable growth and development pains. Already some measurable benefits in terms of pupil achievement have been documented in New Jersey as a result of state activity to explicate the components of a thorough and efficient educational system.[86] Continued state efforts to grapple with educational adequacy issues may focus public attention on the need to specify in precise terms educational goals and objectives that can be translated into programmatic features and state school support schemes.

---

1. *See State Legal Standards for the Provision of Public Education: An Overview* (Washington, D.C.: National Institute of Education, 1978).

2. *See* Arthur Wise, *Legislated Learning* (Berkeley, Calif.: University of California Press, 1979), pp. 12-31; Tyll van Geel, *Authority to Control the School Program* (Lexington, Mass.: D.C. Heath and Company, 1976), Chapter 4.

3. United States Department of Education, *Report on Section 842 State Equalization Plans* (Washington, D.C.: author, 1980). *See also* Orlando Furno, "State Equalization Plans Under Section 842," *Journal of Education Finance* 6, no. 3 (1981):375.

4. *See* Esther Tron, *Public School Finance Programs, 1978-79* (Washington, D.C.: Government Printing Office, 1980), pp. 7-17.

5. *Id.* at 9-17.

6. Fla. Stat. Ann. § 236.081(c)(2)(h).

7. Walter Garms, James Guthrie, and Lawrence Pierce, *School Finance: The Economics and Politics of Public Education* (Englewood Cliffs, N.J.: Prentice-Hall, Inc., 1978), pp. 201-7.

8. Allan Odden and John Augenblick, *School Finance Reform in the States: 1980* (Denver, Colo.: Education Commission of the States, 1980), p. 5.

9. P.L. 88-210 (as amended), 20 U.S.C. § 2301 *et seq.* (1976).

10. Tron, *Public School Finance Programs, 1978-79,* pp. 14-15.

11. In 1980, over $94 million in state aid was earmarked for bilingual/bicultural programs in these 22 states. Odden and Augenblick, *School Finance Reform in the States: 1980,* p. 5.

12. *See* S.C. Code Ann. § 59-20-60(e).

13. In some other states, statutes address the responsibility of local school districts to provide an adequate education but do not prescribe specific programmatic standards. For example, Florida law requires each school district that participates in the state school funding program to "provide evidence of its effort to maintain an adequate school program throughout the district. . ." The statute includes minimum requirements pertaining to accounts and records, school term, personnel employment and salary, budgets, local financial effort, and educational planning, but it does not provide standards for judging program adequacy. Fla. Stat. § 236.02.

14. Ark. Stat. Ann. §§ 80-4601 to 4615.

15. Wis. Stat. Ann. § 121.02 *See* Lee Hansen and F. Howard Nelson, "Impact of the 1973 Wisconsin School Finance Reform," *Selected Papers in School Finance 1978* (Washington, D.C.: Department of Health, Education, and Welfare, 1978), p. 101.

16. Buse v. Smith, 247 N.W.2d 141 (Wis. 1976).

17. Wis. Stat. Ann. § 121.02. In 1979 the Legislature repealed *former* subsections (1)(b), (f), and (m) relating to teacher pay, programs for children with exceptional needs, and minimum school tax levies in certain districts. These items were dealt with elsewhere in the statute. The other minimum standards were retained in this section of the Code. As early as 1949 Wisconsin law stipulated that the state must guarantee basic educational opportunities by providing programs that meet certain quality standards. *See* Hansen and Nelson, "Impact of the 1973 Wisconsin School Finance Reform," p. 112.

18. Ga. Code Ann. § 32-602a.

19. Ga. Code Ann. §§ 32-601a to 672a. *See* Carvin Brown, "Adequate Program for Education in Georgia," *Journal of Education Finance* 3, no. 4 (1978):402-11.

20. N.J. Stat. Ann. § 18A:7A-5. In 1980, the State Board of Education completed its first review of state and local activity to implement the act. The report documented public achievement gains and an increase in compensatory education programs. Also, the report indicated that all districts had completed the development of school outcome goals and were in the process of identifying district and school needs related to the attainment of the goals. Public involvement in education had reportedly increased, and strong citizen advocate groups had been formed. *See* Fred Burke, *The Four-Year Assessment of the Public School Education Act of 1975* (Trenton, N.J.: New Jersey Board of Education, 1980).

21. S. C. Code Ann. §§ 59-20-10 to 59-20-80.

22. Seattle School Dist. No. 1 v. Washington, 585 P.2d 71 (Wash. 1978).

23. Wash. Rev. Code Ann. §§ 28A.58.750 to 760.

24. Va. Const. Art. VIII, § 2. *See* Va. Stat. Ann. § 22.1-18; Acts 1980, c. 667 as amended by Acts 1981, c. 553. Standards are quite specific as to program offerings, staff preparation and development, student testing procedures, pupil-teacher ratios, special education programs, basic skills to be achieved, career preparation, and remedial assistance for underachieving students. *See Standards of Quality for Public Schools in Virginia 1980-82* (Richmond, Va.: Department of Education, 1980).

25. Despite the Virginia Attorney General's opinion stipulating that the legislature must provide sufficient funds for all standards to be met, actual per-pupil appropriations have been below the cost figure calculated by the state education department. *See Report of the Attorney General 1979-80* (Richmond, Va.: Commonwealth of Virginia, 1980), pp. 300-301.

26. W. Va. Code §§ 18-9A-2 to 18-9A-22. *See* Pauley v. Kelly, 255 S.E.2d 859 (W. Va. 1979). *See also* chapter 2, text with note 59.

27. Conn. Gen. Stat. Ann. § 10-16b.

28. *See* Dinah Shelton, "Legislative Control Over Public School Curriculum," *Willamette Law Review* 15 (1979): 475.

29. For example, the North Central Association of Colleges and Schools has standards and guides pertaining to institutional purpose; organization, administration, and control; instructional program; professional staff; pupil personnel services; extra classroom activities; instructional media program; financial support; and school facilities. *See Policies and Standards for the Approval of Secondary Schools 1980-1981* (Boulder, Colo.: North Central Assn. of Colleges and Schools, 1980). There are six private regional accrediting associations: Middle States Association of Colleges and Schools, New England Association of Schools and Colleges, North Central Association of Colleges and Schools, Northwest Association of Schools and Colleges, Southern Association of Colleges and Schools, and Western Association of Schools and Colleges.

30. *NCA Policies and Standards*, p. 3. Usually a task force, with representation from educators across the region, determines what basic minimum standards are

necessary. Drafts of the standards are sent to member schools for reactions and are discussed at state conferences. The task force then rewrites the standards in light of the data collected and presents them to the association governing board for approval. After approval, the standards are sent to all member schools for a vote, and those endorsed by a majority become official standards of the association. Member schools can petition the regional association for a change in standards. If a given standard creates substantial controversy, a research project might be undertaken to ascertain if the standard can be justified.

31. Indiana General Commission on Education, Rule C-1: Curriculum, §§ 2-3 (1978).

32. 704 Kentucky Administrative Regulations 5:050 (1980).

33. Staff Report, "Methods Other States Use to Assure Quality in the Public Schools," Education Review Committee, Ohio General Assembly, Columbus, Ohio, April 1980, p. 5.

34. *Id.* at 10.

35. The Arkansas classification scheme is prescribed by statute, Ark. Stat. Ann. §§ 80-4601 to 4606. In other states, categories usually are identified by the state board of education, and penalties are not associated with the classification scheme as long as minimum standards are met. *See generally*, Department of Education, *Report on Section 842 State Equalization Plans.*

36. Staff Report, "Methods Other States Use to Assure Quality in the Public Schools," p. 11.

37. *Id.* at 12.

38. *See* James Guthrie, "An Assessment of Educational Policy Research," *Educational Evaluation and Policy Analysis* 2, no. 5 (Sept./Oct. 1980); Raymond Callahan, *Education and the Cult of Efficiency* (Chicago: University of Chicago Press, 1962).

39. Phyllis Hawthorne, *Legislation by the States: Accountability and Assessment in Education* (Denver, Colo.: Cooperative Accountability Project, 1974), p. 3.

40. Thomas C. Thomas and Dorothy McKinney, *Accountability in Education* (Menlo Park, Calif.: Stanford University Research Institute, 1972), p. 6.

41. Cooperative Accountability Project, *Accountability in American Education: Will It Make a Difference?* (Denver, Colo. author, 1973), p. 2.

42. Title III of the Elementary and Secondary Education Act of 1965, 20 U.S.C. §§ 841 to 848 (1976), provided categorical aid for supplementary educational centers and services, the establishment of exemplary elementary and secondary programs to serve as models, and the establishment of testing, guidance, and counseling programs.

43. Purposes ascribed to statewide student testing programs have been to assess the adequacy and efficiency of educational programs, to evaluate the effectiveness of schools, and to analyze costs/benefits of particular programs. *See* Maureen

Webster, "Statewide Testing Legislation and Educational Policy," in *Laws, Tests, and Schooling* (Syracuse, N.Y.: Syracuse University Research Corp., 1973), p. 74.

44. Garms, Guthrie, and Pierce, *School Finance: The Economics and Politics of Public Education*, p. 249.

45. Colo. Rev. Stat. § 22-7-102(2)(b).

46. *See* Guthrie, "An Assessment of Educational Policy Research"; Thomas and McKinney, *Accountability in Education*.

47. *See* Guthrie, "An Assessment of Educational Policy Research," p. 48; Wise, *Legislated Learning*, chapter 1; Lawrence Pierce, Walter Garms, James Guthrie, and Michael Kirst, *State School Finance Alternatives* (Eugene, Oreg.: Center for Educational Policy and Management, 1975), chapter 6.

48. Thomas and McKinney, *Accountability in Education*, p. 15.

49. Henry Dyer, "The Role of Evaluation" (paper presented at Educational Testing Service Conference, March 1971), cited in Thomas and McKinney, *Accountability in Education*, p. 16.

50. As a result of the narrow focus, student assessment programs often do not cover areas in which a large portion of instructional time and resources is invested such as abstract reasoning, noncognitive achievement, and creative expression.

51. In Florida, Mississippi, and Maryland, for example, pupil performance objectives are prescribed at the state level.

52. *See* Shirley Boes Neill, *The Competency Movement*, AASA Critical Issues Report (Sacramento, Calif.: Education News Service, 1978).

53. *Id.* at 37. As of 1978, 28 states had used the NAEP model or materials in state assessment programs.

54. *Id.* at 38.

55. *See* Jerome Murphey and David Cohen, "Accountability in Education — The Michigan Experience," *Public Interest* 36 (Summer 1974): 53-81.

56. H. B. 894 § 3(a) (1971), Fla. Stat. Ann. §§ 229.565 and 229.57.

57. H. B. 734 § 11 (1973), Fla. Stat. Ann. §§ 229.55 *et seq.* (as amended).

58. *See* Guthrie, "An Assessment of Educational Policy Research," p. 48; Pierce, Garms, Guthrie, and Kirst, *State School Finance Alternatives*, chapter 6.

59. "Quality Control of Instructional Materials," *Harvard Journal on Legislation* 12, no. 4 (1975):558.

60. By 1974 half of the state legislatures had appropriated funds for career education programs in public schools. Yet most pupil testing programs, used to assess school effectiveness, have not focused on areas such as career education.

61. *See* Fred Burke, *High School Graduation Requirements* (Trenton, N.J.: New Jersey Department of Education, 1979), p. 23; Chris Pipho, *Update VIII: Minimum Competency Testing* (Denver, Colo.: Education Commission of the States, 1978).

62. "Impact of Minimum Competency Testing in Florida," *Today's Education* 67, no. 3 (1978):33.

63. *See generally, Viewpoints in Teaching and Learning* 56, no. 3 (1980).

64. *See* Gordon Cawelti, "National Competency Testing: A Bogus Solution," *Phi Delta Kappan* 49, no. 9 (1978):619.

65. Burke, *High School Graduation Requirements*, p. 23.

66. Staff Report, "Methods Other States Use to Assure Quality in the Public Schools," pp. 13-14.

67. Chris Pipho, *State Activity—Minimal Competency Testing* (Denver, Colo.: Education Commission of the States, 1978).

68. Charles Thomas, "The Minimum Competencies of Minimum Competency Testing," *Viewpoints in Teaching and Learning* 56, no. 3 (1980):30.

69. *See* Barry D. Anderson, *The Costs of Legislated Minimal Competency Requirements* (Denver, Colo.: Education Commission of the States, 1977).

70. *See* Diana Pullin, "Minimum Competency Testing and the Demand for Accountability," *Phi Delta Kappan* 63, no. 1 (1981): 21; "Battle Begins on Minimum Competency Testing," *Education Daily*, 10 July 1981, p. 3; Nathan Glazer, *Affirmative Discrimination: Ethnic Inequality and Public Policy* (New York: Basic Books, 1975). There has also been substantial controversy over the validity and reliability of competency tests used as a prerequisite to the receipt of a high school diploma. *See* George Madaus, "NIE Clarification Hearing: The Negative Team's Case," *Phi Delta Kappan* 63, no. 2 (1981):93-94; Clinton Chase, "Minimal Competency Testing: Are the Instruments Adequate?" *Viewpoints in Teaching and Learning* 56, no. 3 (1980):47-52.

71. *See* Merle McClung, "Competency Testing Programs: Legal and Educational Issues," *Fordham Law Review* 47 (1979): 702. *See also* William Spady, "Competency Based Education: A Bandwagon in Search of a Definition," *Educational Researcher* 6, no. 1, (1977).

72. *See* W. James Popham, "The Case for Minimum Competency Testing," *Phi Delta Kappan* 63, no. 2 (1981):89-91; "Battle Begins on Minimum Competency Testing," p. 4.

73. "Newsfront," *Phi Delta Kappan* 62, no. 8 (1981):547.

74. *See The Book of the States 1980-81* (Lexington, Ky.: Council of State Governments, 1980), p. 352; William Spady, *Literacy: Competency and the Problem of Graduation Requirements* (Washington, D.C.: Office of Education, 1978). *See also Education Daily*, 27 October 1981, p. 6, where it was reported that nearly half of the 24,000 fourth- and seventh-graders who did not satisfy the reading

proficiency standard for promotion in spring 1981 were able to meet the standard after participating in an intensive summer remediation program.

75. Spady, *id.* at 10-13; Popham, "The Case for Minimum Competency Testing," p. 91.

76. "Goals for State Board of Elementary and Secondary Education," Oregon Department of Education, 1981 (mimeographed).

77. *See* David Savage, "Minimum Competencies—The Oregon Approach," *Educational Leadership* 36, no. 1 (1978):13-15; W. R. Nance, "How Fares Competency Development in Oregon?" *Educational Leadership* 35, no. 2 (1977):102-7.

78. Allegations of instructional negligence have not been successful to date. *See* Hoffman v. Board of Educ. of the City of New York, 410 N.Y.S.2d 99 (App. Div. 1978), *rev'd* 424 N.Y.S.2d 376 (Ct. App. 1979); Donohue v. Copiague Union Free Schools, 391 N.E.2d 1352 (N.Y. 1979); Peter W. v. San Francisco Unified School Dist., 131 Cal. Rptr. 854 (Cal. App. 1976). However, if it can be substantiated that schools have failed to teach the required competencies or have erroneously documented that students have acquired the competencies, future plaintiffs may be more successful.

79. Fla. Stat. §§ 232.245(3), 232.246(1)-(3).

80. *See* Dennis Tesolowski, "The Functional Literacy Test: Florida's Approach to Competency Testing," *Viewpoints in Teaching and Learning* 56, no. 3 (1980):71.

81. Debra P. v. Turlington, 644 F.2d 397 (5th Cir. 1981). *See also* Anderson v. Banks, Johnson v. Sikes, 520 F. Supp. 472 (S.D. Ga. 1981).

82. The majority of the research activities have been sponsored by the federal government. *See* Ellis Katz, "Federal Roles in Education," *Compact* 15, no. 2 (1981):30; United States Department of Education *1980 Annual Report* (Washington, D.C.: Department of Education, 1980), p. 6.

83. *See* Stan Shapson, Edgar Wright, Gary Eason, and John Fitzgerald, "An Experimental Study of the Effects of Class Size," *American Educational Research Journal* 17, no. 1 (1980):141-152; Gene Glass and Mary Smith, "Meta-Analysis of Research on Class Size and Achievement," *Educational Evaluation and Policy Analysis* 1, no. 1 (1979):2-16.

84. *See* note 78.

85. *See* Wise, *Legislated Learning*, p. 182. *See also* Betsy Levin, "The Courts, Congress, and Educational Adequacy: The Equal Protection Predicament," *Maryland Law Review* 39 (1979): 256.

86. *See* note 20.

# 4

# Federal Role in Defining
# and Establishing Standards
# of Educational Adequacy

The U.S. Constitution delegates *no* responsibility for education to the federal government, and state constitutions place *total* responsibility for education on state governments. Yet these absolutes are not reflected in reality. The federal government's involvement in public education has been one of indirect influence rather than direct control. Although the U.S. Constitution is silent regarding education, Congress is empowered to enact laws for promoting the general welfare and enforcing constitutional guarantees. Using these powers, the federal government has had a significant impact on educational policies and programs at the local school level. Indeed, federal education regulations have increased over tenfold since 1965.[1] Enforcement activities of federal agencies coupled with judicial interpretations of the laws and regulations have influenced course offerings, methods of instruction, types of curricular material, staff development efforts, student grouping patterns, and other aspects of the public educational enterprise.

Federal involvement in education is not a recent phenomenon. In fact, federal land grants for public schools were authorized prior to ratification of the U.S. Constitution.[2] Over the ensuing years, federal participation in education has evolved into a complex body of legislation and regulations pertaining to approximately 160 individual programs designed to accomplish specific purposes.[3] Judicial activity has provided the impetus for some of these laws, such as the Education for All Handicapped Children Act of 1975, which incorporates actual language from court decisions as to the programs, services, and procedural protections that must be afforded to handicapped pupils.[4] In some instances, areas of educational need have been brought into focus by specific events such as the launching of Sputnik I, resulting in the National Defense Education Act (1958), which was designed to upgrade instruction in science, mathematics, and foreign languages. Other laws have resulted from general dissatisfaction with educational practices. Illustrative is the Family Educational Rights and Privacy Act of 1974, which was intended to remedy abuses in maintaining and disseminating student information. Of course, organized lobbying efforts as well as the philosophical orientations of members of Congress have had a major impact on the substance of federal education laws. Most of the federal initiatives pertaining to elementary and secondary schools have been intended to improve educational equity or quality, and various means, ranging from funding incentives to the imposition of sanctions (i.e., the withdrawal of federal aid), have been used to further these aims.[5]

Two basic types of federal laws (and their accompanying regulations) are especially pertinent to this study because they have directly influenced definitions of educational adequacy and standards by which to assess it. One type pertains to the protection of civil rights, and these laws have been enacted pursuant to congressional authority to enforce the provisions of the Fourteenth Amendment. State and local education agencies must comply with federal civil rights legislation and the accompanying administrative regulations, whereas participation in federal funding programs is optional. Among the civil rights laws affecting school policies and practices are the following: Title VI of the Civil Rights Act of 1964[6] (prohibiting discrimination on the basis of race, color, or national origin in federally-assisted programs or activities), Title VII of the Civil Rights Act of 1964[7] (prohibiting employment discrimination on the basis of race, color, national origin, sex, or religion), Title IX of the Education Amendments of 1972[8] (prohibiting sex discrimination against participants in or beneficiaries of educational programs receiving federal financial assistance), Section 504 of the Rehabilitation Act of 1973[9] (prohibiting discrimination against handicapped persons in federally assisted programs), the Equal Educational Opportunities Act of 1974[10] (mandating equal public educational opportunities without regard to race, color, sex, or national origin), and the Age Discrimination Act of 1975[11] (prohibiting age discrimination in federally assisted programs or activities).

Laws prohibiting discriminatory school practices have given substance to the phrase, "equal educational opportunities." Regulations promulgated pursuant to these laws and court decisions interpreting the provisions have placed affirmative obligations on school districts to provide specific programs and services for certain students to compensate for past disadvantages or present disabilities. The Office of Civil Rights, established in 1966, currently monitors state and local compliance with several of these civil rights acts.[12] While most of these statutes are couched in terms of attaining equity goals under the Fourteenth Amendment equal protection clause, their regulations often include specific standards against which to assess the *adequacy* of educational programs. These provisions have caused changes in student testing procedures, grouping practices, curricular offerings, extracurricular activities, and many other facets of the public school program. These laws not only have altered local school priorities and practices, they also, in many cases, have stimulated state legislation modeled after the federal mandates.

The second general type of federal legislation pertinent to this study consists of categorical aid programs that provide funding incentives to state and local education agencies for the improvement of educational programs and services in light of nationally recognized priorities. Congress has justified such categorical funding laws with the rationale that states and local communities, on their own initiative, have not adequately addressed certain curricular areas and special student needs.[13] In 1980, 94% of the nation's public school districts received some type of federal categorical aid, with most districts participating in at least two programs.[14]  The largest categorical programs provide aid to upgrade educational opportunities for culturally and educationally disadvantaged and handicapped children and to improve vocational and technical education, but there are numerous smaller categorical programs covering such topics as Indian education, career education, delinquency prevention, reading improvement, educational television, food services, and research and dissemination activities.[15] While states have the option of not participating in these categorical programs, if they do accept the federal aid, they must comply with the accompanying guidelines.

The detailed regulations accompanying both civil rights and categorical aid laws have generated substantial tension between the federal government and state and local education agencies. It has been alleged that such extensive federal specifications as to what must be taught and how it must be delivered usurp state and local prerogatives in determining the components of the curriculum.[16] It also has been charged that compliance efforts among various federal programs are not coordinated, resulting in paperwork duplications and even conflicting program requirements.[17] In defense of the federal regulations, it has been argued that extensive monitoring is necessary to ensure that federal funds are not diverted from their intended purposes. It also has been asserted that detailed regulations are necessary, particularly in connection with civil rights legislation, because states have been recalcitrant in altering discriminatory practices.[18]

In the following five sections of this chapter, we examine selected federal laws and regulations, noting their impact on definitions and standards of educational adequacy. Specifically, we look at federal initiatives pertaining to special education, bilingual education, compensatory education, vocational education, and research and development activities. In a concluding section, we offer some observations as to the future federal role in establishing standards of educational adequacy for public schools.

# Special Education for Handicapped Students

Since the latter 1950s, federal funds have been available through various categorical programs to assist state and local education agencies in training teachers of the handicapped and upgrading special education programs and services.[19] While participation in such programs has been discretionary, in 1973 Congress enacted civil rights legislation on behalf of the handicapped. Section 504 of the Rehabilitation Act of 1973 prohibits recipients of federal financial assistance from discriminating against an otherwise qualified handicapped person solely on the basis of the handicap.[20] It bars employment discrimination against the handicapped in connection with recruitment, selection, compensation, job assignment and classification, and fringe benefits. It also requires that newly constructed facilities be accessible to the handicapped. It does not mandate that all existing facilities be remodeled, but all *programs* must be readily accessible to handicapped persons. Section 504 also prohibits discrimination against the handicapped in postsecondary education and requires public education agencies to provide a free appropriate education for all handicapped children in the least restrictive environment.

This last requirement is closely coordinated with the provisions of Public Law 94-142, the Education for All Handicapped Children Act of 1975, which is a funding law that provides federal assistance to defray some of the excess costs associated with providing a free appropriate education for handicapped children.[21] Because of its relationship with Section 504, P.L. 94-142 has been interpreted as creating rights as well as constituting a source of federal funds. The most precise federal requirements as to program adequacy for special-need students have emanated from this 1975 act. Indeed, P.L. 94-142, in conjunction with Section 504, requires more than minimum educational adequacy for handicapped children and stipulates that educational programs must be *appropriate* to meet these pupils' identified special education needs.

Under the provisions of P.L. 94-142, state and local education agencies are to give first priority to locating previously unserved handicapped children and providing them with appropriate programs. As a result, extensive "child find" campaigns have been initiated in many states. The next priority under the law is to upgrade programs for students being served inadequately. The law stipulates that the federal aid can only be used to assist with excess costs associated with such special education services; it cannot be used to supplant state and local funds.[22]

Public Law 94-142 is unprecedented in that it requires state and local education agencies to assure program adequacy for handicapped students and specifies the form that such assurances must take. For example, the mandated individualized educational program (IEP) is one strategy to guarantee that appropriate instruction is provided for handicapped children in the least restrictive environment. The IEP must be designed by a planning team, including the child's regular teacher, specialized personnel, the child's parent or guardian, and if possible the child. The program must contain goals for the handicapped child, short-term and long-range objectives to attain the goals, specification of the services that will be provided, and an evaluation schedule.

The due process requirements contained in P.L. 94-142 represent another mechanism to ensure educational adequacy. Handicapped children and their parents are guaranteed elaborate procedural safeguards prior to any change in a child's instructional assignment. Thus "procedural adequacy" must be provided in connection with all placement decisions. Some courts have even held that the suspension of a handicapped child for disciplinary reasons constitutes a program change that must be accompanied by procedures to determine an alternative more appropriate placement for the child.[23] The rationale for these extensive due process requirements is that they will deter improper placements and permanent assignments to special classes or schools.

In contrast to the specificity of P.L. 94-142 in regard to the development of IEPs for handicapped children and procedural safeguards that must be followed in making placement changes, the act does not specify the particular components of the programs that must be provided. Such components are expected to vary depending on each child's deficiencies. The act stipulates that handicapped children are entitled to specially designed instruction, at no cost to parents or guardians, to meet their unique needs, "including classroom instruction, instruction in education, home instruction, and instruction in hospitals and institutions."[24] Furthermore, education agencies must provide related services such as transportation and developmental, corrective, and other supportive services necessary for a child to benefit from special education.[25] Questions persist, however, as to exactly what programs and services must be provided in order to satisfy these federal requirements. Thus courts are being called upon to interpret what constitutes an appropriate education.

It seems clear that "appropriate" means more than merely providing access to *some* educational opportunity. However, it is unlikely that this mandate means that each handicapped child is entitled to the *best* possible program available. What remains controversial is where on the continuum between these extremes lies the acceptable interpretation. As discussed in chapter two, several courts have given broad interpretation to the statutory protections, thereby placing many new responsibilities on state and local education agencies.[26] Judicial interpretations of what constitutes an appropriate education for handicapped pupils have influenced grouping practices, disciplinary procedures, staffing patterns, and a host of other traditionally local concerns.

In response primarily to the federal mandates on behalf of the handicapped, the Council of Chief State School Officers has labeled the federal government a "super school board" that is specifying not only educational goals but also specific means that must be used to attain the goals.[27] Some state officials have charged that the federal government's priorities are not consistent with state and local priorities and that federal laws and regulations are imposing responsibilities on schools that possibly should be assigned to other public agencies.[28]

Although most states have modeled statutory mandates after the federal legislation on behalf of the handicapped, it appears that such state action has often been the direct result of federal pressure. In no other domain has the federal government's role in establishing specific program requirements been as pervasive as it has been in connection with handicapped pupils. State and local education agencies have been left little discretion in determining how such children will be served. The federal legislation and regulations (in concert with court decisions interpreting these mandates) have placed extensive programmatic and fiscal obligations upon public schools.

## Bilingual Education

Federal mandates on behalf of English-deficient children also have gone beyond requirements of *equal* treatment and have stipulated that children with English language deficiencies are entitled to *special* assistance because of their unique needs. Since 1968 federal categorical funds have been available to assist school districts in designing and implementing programs for English-deficient students.[29] Such efforts were strengthened by the Equal Educational Opportunities Act of 1974, which stipulates that "the failure of an educational agency to take appropriate action to overcome language barriers that impede equal participation by its students in its instructional programs" is an unlawful denial of equal educational opportunity.[30] Regulations for the act specify that instruction in the child's native language must be provided in all subjects to the extent necessary for the child to progress through the educational system and master the English language.

Also, the U.S. Supreme Court ruled in *Lau* v. *Nichols* that Title VI of the Civil Rights Act of 1964, which prohibits discrimination on the basis of race, color, or national origin in any activity that receives federal financial assistance, entitles non-English-speaking students to special instructional assistance in mastering the English language.[31] In response to this Supreme Court ruling, the Department of Health, Education and Welfare issued informal guidelines, known as the *Lau* Remedies, to aid local schools in designing programs for children with limited ability to speak English. Controversy has continued, however, as to precisely what obligations are placed on school districts to meet the needs of English-deficient children. Must bilingual/bicultural programs be provided or will the provision of compensatory English instruction satisfy legal requirements?[32]

In 1980 the Department of Education proposed regulations pursuant to Title VI in an attempt to clarify the responsibilities placed on school districts to provide appropriate programs for these pupils.[33] The proposed *Lau* Rules required transitional bilingual instruction to be provided for children with severe English deficiencies. For students with some mastery of the English language, either bilingual education or compensatory English instruction could be provided. It was estimated that implementation of the regulations would cost school districts between \$200 and \$400 million a year in addition to federal and state funds already being spent on bilingual education.[34]

The *Lau* Rules created substantial controversy in educational and legislative forums as to the Department of Education's authority to place specific program requirements upon public schools. National education associations charged that the proposed regulations would subvert the authority of local school districts to design the curriculum and possibly set a dangerous precedent as to future federal regulation of *what* constitutes adequate instruction and *how* such instruction must be provided.[35] Congress also voiced concern over the *Lau* Rules by attaching riders to bills stipulating that the Department of Education could not issue final bilingual regulations until June 1981 to provide lawmakers sufficient time to study the issue.[36] In February 1981, reacting to massive negative sentiment, Education Secretary Terrel Bell withdrew the controversial proposed rules, which he called "inflexible, unworkable, and incredibly costly."[37]

The withdrawal of the *Lau* Rules has elicited mixed responses. It has been assailed by civil rights activists as a sign that federal regulatory agencies under the Reagan administration intend to be less assertive in promulgating regulations to protect the civil rights of students.[38] Professional education associations have applauded the move as a victory for advocates of local control.[39] Although Secretary Bell has offered verbal assurances that the Department of Education will continue to protect the rights of English-deficient students, he has indicated that the department will promulgate fewer and less cumbersome regulations.

## Compensatory Education

The Elementary and Secondary Education Act of 1964 (ESEA) represented the first major involvement of the federal government in providing financial assistance to public schools.[40] The largest portion of ESEA funds, contained in Title I, was earmarked to assist school districts with "concentrations of children from low-income families" in addressing the "special educational needs of educationally deprived children."[41] Other titles of the original act and subsequent amendments have provided funds for library resources, textbooks, and instructional materials; supplemental education centers and services; research and training efforts; activities to strengthen state education agencies; basic skill improvement programs; and special services and programs for the handicapped, English-deficient, and other groups of children with special needs. After passage of the ESEA, federal appropriations tripled between 1965 and 1966.

Title I signaled federal recognition that poor children need additional resources and compensatory instruction in order to receive an adequate education. To be eligible for Title I funds, school districts must comply with detailed program specifications. Local districts must assess the special needs of educationally deprived pupils, assign priorities to these needs, and develop a plan (which must receive state approval) to meet the needs. Title I also requires school districts to substantiate that local expenditures in Title I schools are comparable to those in non-Title I schools. This requirement is intended to ensure that federal funds supplement rather than supplant local and state funds.

About half of the states have followed the federal lead in earmarking state aid for compensatory education programs. Guidelines for local districts have been modeled after the federal regulations in some states. Most of the compensatory programs have concentrated on basic skill development in reading and mathematics, because these have been identified as the areas of greatest need among the target students.[42] Without question, the federal government has had a significant impact on the development of criteria to assess program adequacy for culturally and educationally deprived students.

In some instances school districts have been required to provide compensatory instructional programs (with or without federal financial assistance) to fulfill federal constitutional and statutory obligations to minority students who have been the victims of past discrimination. In 1977 the U.S. Supreme Court specifically recognized the authority of the federal judiciary to place such instructional requirements on school districts.[43] It approved lower court rulings that required programs in remedial reading and communciation skills, counseling and career guidance, inservice teacher training, and nondiscriminatory testing as part of the desegregation plan for the Detroit school system. Following this decision, compensatory programs have been required in desegregation plans for numerous school districts, including Wilmington,

Delaware, and Cleveland, Ohio.[44] Recently, the judiciary has reflected the sentiment that student reassignment alone cannot counteract the effects of discriminatory practices; minority students have a federal right to instructional programs that adequately address their educational deficiencies.

Title IV of the Civil Rights Act of 1964[45] and the Emergency School Aid Act of 1972[46] also have encouraged the establishment of compensatory education programs in schools undergoing court-ordered or voluntary desegregation. Under both acts, federal funds are available to assist in providing such programs. However, the funds may not be released to any school district if it has policies or procedures (such as pupil grouping practices) that result in discrimination based on race. Thus these legislative acts not only have encouraged the provision of compensatory education but also have required school districts to eliminate certain discriminatory practices.

## Vocational Education

The provision of funds to upgrade vocational and technical education has been a long-standing federal priority.[47] Federal aid has been made available through various acts; the Vocational Education Act of 1963 has been the largest source of funds for elementary and secondary education.[48] To receive aid under this act, states must develop five-year plans for federal approval and submit annual reports specifying objectives and detailing progress in meeting the objectives. Each state must establish a system to monitor the law's implementation, including its prohibition against sex discrimination in vocational education. At the local level advisory councils must assess the vocational education needs of the community and develop an instructional plan to meet those needs. In distributing federal funds, states must give priority to economically depressed areas and school districts with high unemployment rates or concentrations of low-income families or special-need students.[49] The funds may not be used for any program that does not prepare students for employment or assist them in making informed vocational and career choices. Funding priorities include the construction of vocational facilities, advancement of equity goals, and curriculum development.

In 1980 the Office of Vocational and Adult Education, which administers the 1963 act and vocational programs included in various other laws, reported that almost 20 million persons received some type of vocational training in federally assisted programs.[50] The federal emphasis on vocational education has stimulated considerable state activity as well. State specifications as to program adequacy in the area of vocational education are more detailed than in many other curricular areas because of the planning and monitoring activities required by the federal regulations.  Moreover, state and local funding for vocational education almost tripled from 1972 to 1979, even though federal aid for vocational education increased less than 50% during this same time period.[51]

# Research, Development, and Dissemination Activities

Federal research, development, and dissemination efforts often have indirectly influenced definitions and standards of educational adequacy at state and local levels.  The Department of Education's Office of Educational Research and Improvement (OERI) operates over 40 programs that support research to improve the quality of education, particularly for students with special needs.[52]  One component of OERI is the National Center for Education Statistics (NCES), which collects statistical data on the condition and quality of American education.[53]  Such data are analyzed to identify trends, problems, and policy issues needing federal, state, or local attention.  Another OERI unit is the National Diffusion Network, which emphasizes the installation of innovative educational programs of proven effectiveness.  This network funded 79 basic skills projects in 1980 to disseminate to schools and colleges information about exemplary new approaches to teaching and learning.[54]

The National Institute of Education (NIE) was established in 1972 to provide leadership in research and development activities, to advance educational equity goals, and to improve educational practices at the local district level.[55]  Through contracts and grants, NIE has funded numerous research projects, such as the Effective Schools Project, to investigate why certain schools are successful in raising student achievement scores.[56]  Also, the NIE Big-City School Superintendents' Network on Urban Education has provided a forum for superintendents to discuss and seek solutions to common problems.[57]  Another responsibility assigned to NIE is to conduct a regular assessment of student achievement; this is carried out through a contractual arrangement with the Education Commission of the States to administer the National Assessment of Educational Progress (NAEP).[58]  Such assessment data, as well as the NAEP objectives and test items, have been used in establishing state and local standards for pupil performance in designing assessment programs.

Perhaps a more subtle federal influence on standards of educational adequacy has resulted from its sponsorship of curriculum development and dissemination projects.  For example, through the National Science Foundation (NSF), the federal government has sponsored curriculum development projects since 1957.[59]  While the intent of these projects has not been to impose a national curriculum on local school districts, such federally supported curriculum materials possibly have a competitive advantage because they can be marketed at a lower cost than materials without federal support and because they carry an inference of federal endorsement.[60] Curricular programs such as "Science—A Process Approach" and "Man—A Course of Study," developed through NSF grants, have been widely adopted by school districts. These programs emphasize particular instructional strategies as well as value orientations.

Also illustrative of federally sponsored development activities are those funded under the Women's Educational Equity Act (WEEA), which has supported development, demonstration, and dissemination projects to advance equity for women.[61] Model projects to eliminate education barriers for women, to enhance Title IX compliance, and to reduce sex-role stereotyping have had an impact on the public school curriculum and have resulted in changes in school policies and practices to eliminate sex bias.

Federal funds have been made available for other targeted educational research and development efforts, some administered by OERI and others administered by the Office of Elementary and Secondary Education. For example, Section 842 of the Education Amendments of 1974 provided funds to assist states in assessing the condition of school finance systems and in designing new approaches to achieve greater equalization of resources among school districts.[62] Many categorical aid programs in areas such as career education, Indian education, metric education, environmental education, gifted and talented education, and educational telecommunications have contained research, development, and dissemination components.[63] Data from such research activities have been used to make educational program modifications, sometimes on a statewide basis. Indeed, it has been asserted that almost all educational innovations since the latter 1960s have resulted from federal research and development initiatives.[64]

## Future Federal Role

To date, the major federal activity in defining and establishing standards of educational adequacy for public schools has pertained to special-need students and targeted curricular areas. The federal government has not attempted to prescribe the components of an adequate general education that must be assured all children within this nation. However, federal laws, agency regulations, and court decrees interpreting the federally protected rights of special-need students have influenced state legislation, including school finance schemes. For example, all states have enacted legislation or administrative regulations, modeled after the federal mandates, that guarantee the rights of handicapped pupils to receive special education services. Every state also has included some provision for such programs in state aid formulas. Indeed, the three programs most often receiving targeted state aid—special education, compensatory education, and vocational education—represent federal priorities.

Possibly, the federal mandates outlining the components of an adequate education for special-need students may stimulate similar specificity in delineating the components of a basic or adequate education for *all* pupils. Moreover, some of the services currently required for handicapped students may be prescribed for the nonhandicapped as well. A double standard is operating at present, in that the adequacy of the regular school program usually is judged by minimum input standards. Yet programs for special-need students must be more than minimally sufficient; they must be *appropriate* to meet the needs of the learner. This "individual needs" orientation toward determining what constitutes an adequate education represents another perspective in addition to the input and output approaches.

If states should follow the federal lead and adopt a needs-based definition of adequacy, it is conceivable that nonhandicapped as well as handicapped children in the future might be entitled to individualized educational programs (IEPs), year-round instruction if needed, and special services to "maximize their learning potential."[65] Already a small school system in Nebraska has reported positive results from its use of IEPs for all pupils within the district.[66] Nebraska has made state funds available for other school systems that wish to implement such a program. Also, a Wisconsin statute suggests, but does not require, that the equivalent of an IEP be developed for truant students,[67] and in New Jersey an individualized improvement plan is required for students identified as deficient in the basic skills.[68] If state legislatures ultimately should specify that school districts must provide *appropriate programs* to meet the unique needs of *all pupils* (as currently required for only certain special-need children), a substantial increase in educational funds would be required. Also, far more sophisticated pupil weighting schemes would be necessary so that funding formulas could accurately reflect the costs associated with addressing the complete range of students' needs.

It seems likely, however, that the federal role in public education may be reduced or at least refocused during the coming decade. Thus continuing federal leadership in championing school access and educational equity for all children cannot be assured. Several recent actions by the Department of Education have provided signals that the federal government intends to take a more conservative approach to promulgating and enforcing civil rights regulations. For example, the department's withdrawal of the *Lau* Rules has been assailed by civil rights groups.[69] Similarly, the department's recent decision to reconsider the validity of its regulations protecting educational employees from sex bias under Title IX of the Education Amendments of 1972 has been viewed as a retreat in the civil rights areas.[70] Also, pursuant to Executive Order 12291, in 1981 the department began reviewing regulations for P.L. 94-142 and Section 504 of the Rehabilitation Act of 1973 to identify overly prescriptive provisions and reduce the burdens and costs of federal regulatory activity.[71] It appears that the Department of Education, or its noncabinet-level successor, will place fewer and less restrictive civil rights requirements on state and local education agencies.

The movement to convert federal education aid from categorical to block grants also has implications for the future federal role in establishing priorities and standards of program adequacy for public schools. The Reagan administration proposed the consolidation of 44 categorical programs into two block grants.[72] While Congress made substantial modifications in the administration's proposal for fiscal year 1982, in its original form the consolidation plan would have provided federal funds for states with few restrictions as to their use. The plan's underlying assumption was that states have now enacted legislation consistent with federal priorities, so extensive federal monitoring is no longer required.[73] The proposed plan would have dramatically altered the federal government's involvement in establishing programmatic specifications for public schools.

The modified block grant plan adopted by Congress for fiscal year 1982 maintains the major elementary and secondary categorical programs intact. The block grant excludes Title I programs, the Education for All Handicapped Children Act, vocational and adult education, and impact aid. However, 28 smaller categorical programs are combined in grants to the states, 80% of which must flow through the states to local education agencies. Unlike the Reagan proposal, the modified plan maintains restrictions on the use of the federal aid. There is some sentiment that the adopted plan contains the worst of both worlds in that federal aid has been reduced but federal red tape and restrictions have been retained.[74]

Although Congress has not yet been persuaded to convert all categorical aid for education into block grants, movement in this direction, already begun, seems likely to continue. If such federal block grants ultimately should be awarded to state and local education agencies without restrictions as to the use of the funds, the federal role in establishing social policy—including standards of educational adequacy—through categorical grants might diminish significantly. Assuming that the federal government does disengage itself somewhat from the educational domain, interpretation and enforcement of state law will become even more pivotal in delineating the scope of students' rights to an adequate education.

Without federal pressure and incentives to provide appropriate programs for certain types of pupils, states may also modify their provisions pertaining to special-need students. In a period of increasing financial constraints, it cannot be assumed that state and local education agencies will maintain their commitment to targeted pupils and curricular areas without the federal impetus.[75]

There is some sentiment, however, that federal involvement in education will continue, with a change in focus. Priorities such as student achievement in basic skills and support for private education might replace the recent equity and access thrusts.[76] Secretary Bell has observed that in attempting to ensure equal opportunity and access to education, literacy and academic competency have declined. He has encouraged local districts to adopt policies establishing "maximum competency tests" for students and rewards for teachers to challenge students and teachers to reach their highest potential.[77] Also, in August 1981, Bell announced the formation of a National Commission on Excellence in Education. The commission's charge is to examine and compare curriculum, standards, and expectations for schools in this country and other countries and to hold public hearings on how to foster excellence in American education.[78]

It is possible that the general education program (instead of targeted programs) will feel the major federal influence during the 1980s. Efforts to establish national competency standards for students may receive additional support. If the federal government does move into the domain of establishing output specifications for the general education program, state definitions and standards of educational adequacy could be significantly affected. This might promote a change from the current input orientation to an outcome approach in defining the state's educational obligations.

1.  Arthur Wise, *Legislated Learning* (Berkeley, Calif.: University of California Press, 1979), p. 2.

2.  Federal land grants for public schools were authorized by the Congress of the Confederation in 1785. *See* W. Vance Grant and Leo Eiden, *The Digest of Education Statistics, 1980* (Washington, D.C.: National Center for Education Statistics, 1980), p. 175.

3.  United States Department of Education, *1980 Annual Report* (Washington, D.C.: Department of Education, 1980), p. 4.

4. P.L. 94-142, 20 U.S.C. § 1401 *et seq.* (1976). *See* Mills v. Board of Educ. of the District of Columbia, 348 F. Supp. 866 (D.D.C. 1972).

5. Michael Kirst has identified the following ways that higher levels of government can influence lower levels in the provision of services such as education: general aid, differential funding, regulation, research and dissemination of knowledge, provision of services, and exertion of moral persuasion. *See* Michael Kirst, "The Future Federal Role in Education: Parties, Candidates, and the 1975 Elections," *Phi Delta Kappan* 58, no. 2 (1976):155.

6. P.L. 88-352, 42 U.S.C. § 2000d-2000d-4 (1976). Title IV of the same act authorizes assistance to school boards, states, municipalities, school districts, or other units of government in the preparation, adoption, and implementation of plans for school desegregation. Technical assistance and funds are made available to employ specialized educational personnel, to provide inservice training, and to establish other types of programs to address problems incident to desegregation. *See* 42 U.S.C. § 2000c-2000c-9 (1976).

7. P.L. 88-352, 42 U.S.C. § 2000e-2000e-17 (1976). *See also* the Equal Pay Act of 1963, P.L. 88-38, 29 U.S.C. § 206 (1976), which prohibits discrimination on the basis of sex in wages and fringe benefits.

8. P.L. 92-318, Education Amendments of 1972, 20 U.S.C. § 1681 (1976).

9. P.L. 93-112, 29 U.S.C § 794 (1976).

10. P.L. 93-380, 20 U.S.C. § 1701 (1976).

11. P.L. 94-135, 42 U.S.C. § 6101 (1976).

12. *See* United States Department of Education, *1980 Annual Report,* pp. 70-74.

13. Stafford Smiley, "The Elementary and Secondary Education Amendments of 1974: The Effect of the Consolidation and Review Provisions Upon the Distribution of Decisionmaking Authority," *Harvard Journal on Legislation* 12, no. 3 (1975): 450-53.

14. Nancy Dearman and Valena Plisko, *Condition of Education 1980* (Washington, D.C.: National Center for Education Statistics, 1980), p. 61. The majority of school districts receive funds under Title I of the Elementary and Secondary Education Act of 1965 and P.L. 94-142, the Education for All Handicapped Children Act of 1975.

15. *See* United States Department of Education, *1980 Annual Report.*

16. *See Education Daily,* 3 September 1980, p. 3; Smiley, "The Elementary and Secondary Education Amendments of 1974," p. 452. *See also,* Tyll van Geel, *Authority to Control the School Program* (Lexington, Mass.: D.C. Heath and Company, 1976), p. 2 and chapter 3.

17. *See* Beryl Radin, "Equal Educational Opportunity and Federalism," In *Government in the Classroom,* ed. Mary F. Williams (Montpelier, Vt.: Capital City Press, 1979), pp. 77-86.

18. *See Education Daily*, 3 February 1981, p. 2; Smiley, "The Elementary and Secondary Education Amendments of 1974," pp. 493-94.

19. For example, in 1958 the Education of Mentally Retarded Children Act (P.L. 85-926) authorized the use of federal funds to train teachers for handicapped children. In 1966 the Elementary and Secondary Education Amendments (P.L. 89-750) authorized federal grants to assist states in the initiation, expansion, and improvement of programs and projects for handicapped preschool, elementary, and secondary pupils. The Handicapped Children's Early Education Assistance Act of 1968 (P.L. 90-538) authorized preschool and early education programs for handicapped children.

20. P.L. 93-112, 29 U.S.C. § 794 (1976).

21. P.L. 94-142, 20 U.S.C. § 1401 (1976).

22. P.L. 94-142, 20 U.S.C. § 1414 (a)(1), (a)(2)(B)(i) (1976). *See also* 45 C.F.R. § 121a.182 (1980).

23. *See* S-1 v. Turlington, 635 F.2d 342 (5th Cir. 1981), *cert. denied*, 102 S. Ct. 566 (1981); Southeast Warren Community School Dist. v. Department of Public Instruction, 285 N.W.2d 173 (Iowa 1979); Stuart v. Nappi, 443 F. Supp. 1235 (D. Conn. 1978).

24. P.L. 94-142, 20 U.S.C. § 1401(16) (1976).

25. P.L. 94-142, 20 U.S.C. § 1401(17) (1976). *See also* 45 C.F.R. § 121a.13 (1979).

26. *See* chapter 2, text with note 83.

27. Council of Chief State School Officers, *Impediments to Effective Federal-State Relations*, Legislative Meeting, Washington, D.C., March 6-8, 1977 (ED 139110).

28. *See* United States Office of Education and Education Commission of the States, *State Leadership and the Federal Presence in Education* (Denver, Colo.: United States Department of Health, Education, and Welfare, 1979).

29. *See* P.L. 90-247, Bilingual Education Act of 1968, 20 U.S.C. § 880b to 880b-6 (1976). *See also*, The Emergency School Aid Act of 1972, P.L. 92-318, 20 U.S.C. § 1601 (1976).

30. P.L. 93-380, Title II, 20 U.S.C. § 1703(f) (1976).

31. 414 U.S. 563 (1974).

32. *See* Guadalupe Organization, Inc. v. Tempe Elementary School Dist. No. 3, 587 F.2d 1022 (9th Cir. 1978); Keyes v. School Dist. No. 1, 521 F.2d 465 (10th Cir. 1975); Morales v. Shannon, 516 F.2d 411 (5th Cir. 1975); Aspira v. Board of Educ. of the City of New York, No. 4002 (S.D.N.Y. 1974); United States v. Texas, 342 F. Supp. 24 (E.D. Tex. 1971), *aff'd*, 466 F.2d 518 (5th Cir. 1972). *See also* chapter 2, text with note 79.

33. *Federal Register* 45, no. 152 (August 5, 1980).

34. "NSBA Opposes Bilingual Education Regulation," *Indiana School Boards Association Journal* 26, no. 5, (1980):26.

35. At least ten national education groups charged that the Department of Education acted beyond the intent of Title VI in designing the *Lau* Rules. The Rules were attacked as subverting local control and eliminating options available to local administrators and school boards in developing instructional programs. *See Education Daily*, 3 September 1980, p. 3.

36. *See Education Daily*, 7 November 1980, p. 5.

37. *Education Daily*, 3 February 1981, p. 1.

38. *Id.* at 2.

39. *Id.*

40. P.L. 89-10, 20 U.S.C. § 241a (1976).

41. 20 U.S.C. § 241a (1976).

42. Office of Evaluation and Dissemination, *Annual Evaluation Report on Programs Administered by the U.S. Office of Education: 1979* (Washington, D.C.: Department of Health, Education, and Welfare, 1979), pp. 99 and 110.

43. Milliken v. Bradley (Milliken II), 433 U.S. 267 (1977).

44. *See* Evans v. Buchanan, 447 F. Supp. 982 (D. Del. 1978); Reed v. Rhodes, 455 F. Supp. 546, 569 (N.D. Ohio 1978).

45. P.L. 88-352, 42 U.S.C. § 2000c-2000c-9 (1976).

46. P.L. 92-318, 20 U.S.C. § 1601 (1976).

47. Congress has enacted legislation providing assistance for vocational education since 1917 when it passed the Smith-Hughes Act. For a list of these laws, *see* Grant and Eiden, *The Digest of Education Statistics 1980*, pp. 175-80.

48. P.L. 88-210, 20 U.S.C. § 1241. This act has been amended over the years. Major revisions were made in the Education Amendments of 1976, P.L. 94-482, 20 U.S.C. § 2301 (1976).

49. 20 U.S.C. 2306 (1976).

50. United States Department of Education, *1980 Annual Report*, p. 53.

51. National Center for Education Statistics, *The Condition of Vocational Education 1981* (Washington, D.C.: Department of Education, 1981).

52. United States Department of Education, *1980 Annual Report*, pp. 61-69.

53. *See* Iris Garfield, *The Condition of Education, Part 2 1980* (Washington, D.C.: National Center for Education Statistics, 1980).

54. United States Department of Education, *1980 Annual Report,* pp. 66-67.

55. *Id.* at 62-64.

56. *Id.* at 64.

57. *Id.* at 68.

58. *See* Shirley Boes Neill, *The Competency Movement: Problems and Solutions* (Sacramento, Calif.: Education News Service for American Association of School Administrators, 1978), pp. 33-40. *See also,* chapter 3, text with note 52.

59. *See* van Geel, *Authority to Control the School Program,* pp. 66-70.

60. *Id.* at 67-69.

61. P.L. 93-380, 20 U.S.C. § 1866 (1976). *See also Women's Educational Equity Act Program Annual Report 1980* (Washington, D.C.: Department of Education, 1980).

62. P.L. 93-380 § 842, 20 U.S.C. § 246 (1976).

63. *See* House Committee on Education and Labor, *A Compilation of Federal Education Laws* (Washington, D.C.: Government Printing Office, 1981); Office of Evaluation and Dissemination, *Annual Evaluation Report on Programs Administered by the United States Office of Education: 1979* (Washington, D.C.: Government Printing Office, 1979).

64. Katz, "Federal Roles in Education," p. 30.

65. For a discussion of the rights of handicapped children to appropriate programs and services, see chapter 2, text with note 83.

66. *See Education U.S.A.* 23, no. 3 (15 September 1980):18.

67. Warren L. Kruenen, "The Law and the Handicapped Student" (paper presented at the National Organization on Legal Problems of Education Annual Convention, Boston, Mass., 14 November 1980).

68. Fred G. Burke, *Guidelines for High School Graduation Requirements* (Trenton, N.J.: New Jersey State Department of Education, 1980), p. 5. An Individual Student Improvement Plan (ISIP) is required for any student exhibiting basic skill deficiencies in the sixth grade.

69. *See Education Daily,* 3 February 1981, p. 2.

70. *See Education Daily,* 10 September 1981, p. 3. *See also* "Newsnotes," *Phi Delta Kappan* 63, no. 6 (1982):426.

71. *See* Office of Special Education, "Briefing Paper: Initial Review of Regulations Under Part B of the Handicapped Act, As Amended," United States Department of Education, 1 September 1981.

72. *See* David Florio, "Legislation," *Viewpoints in Teaching and Learning* 57, no. 2 (1981):138-42.

73. *See Education Daily*, 29 May 1981, p. 5.

74. *See Education Daily*, 11 June 1981, p. 2.

75. In January 1982 President Reagan proposed that several federal education programs, including vocational and adult education and the school lunch program, be turned over to the states under his "new federalism" policy. Some education programs such as compensatory education (Title I), Head Start, and education of the handicapped would continue to be administered by the federal government, presumably by a foundation that would replace the Education Department. *See Education Times* 3, no. 2 (1982):1.

76. David L. Clark and Mary Anne Amiot, "The Impact of the Reagan Administration on Federal Educational Policy," *Phi Delta Kappan* 63, no. 4 (1981):258-59.

77. *See Education Daily*, 31 August 1981, p. 1.

78. *See Education Daily*, 27 August 1981, p. 1.

# 5
# Conclusion

The school finance reform movement has evolved into an educational reform movement, with mounting support for the notion that equalization of resources alone cannot remedy deficiencies in state educational systems. Courts, legislatures, and administrative agencies have become concerned about whether instructional programs are sufficient to attain state educational goals. Educational policy makers considered knowledgeable in the area of school finance, responding to a national survey in 1980, reported that adequacy issues were the most pressing problems in financing public schools.[1] The quest for educational adequacy has generated substantial legal activity; however, the meaning of the term "adequacy" has eluded consensus. The key question is no longer whether educational adequacy will be addressed but, rather, how it will be defined, measured, and translated into funding schemes.

In the first section of this chapter we summarize major points from the preceding three chapters. Then we explore briefly some obstacles to defining and assuring an adequate education. In this concluding section we offer a few observations on future judicial, legislative, and administrative directions with respect to educational adequacy.

## Summary of Legal Activity

What, legally, is an adequate education? Courts, legislative bodies, and administrative agencies have not yet provided a complete answer to this question. The law is still evolving, and only a few state legislatures have directly defined the components of the educational program that must be guaranteed by the state. Nonetheless, partial definitions of what constitutes an adequate education (in terms of resources, offerings, and/or outcomes) can be gleaned from various state and federal laws and regulations that prescribe standards for schools and from judicial interpretations of constitutional and statutory provisions. The following generalizations are supported by the legislative, administrative, and judicial mandates analyzed in this study.

### Litigation

1. The U.S. Supreme Court has inferred that there is a federal constitutional entitlement to *some* education (necessary for the exercise of free expression and participation in the political process), but has deferred to state legislatures to determine the *level* of education that must be assured by the

states. Also, federal courts have ruled that there is no right under the Fourteenth Amendment equal protection clause to equity in educational resources, programs, tax burden, or outcomes.

2. All state constitutions contain explicit language pertaining to the legislative duty to provide for public education, but state courts have varied considerably in interpreting the scope of this obligation.

3. In some states, courts have concluded that as long as the legislature makes some provision for a *minimum* education for all students (e.g., a minimum foundation program), legislative discretion should be respected in deciding how much education will be provided and how it will be supported. In these states, legislatures often have given substantial latitude to local school districts to determine what constitutes an adequate education.

4. In other states an adequate education has been judicially defined in terms of *equity* in tax burden and educational revenues. Legislatures have been required to devise school support systems that are fiscally neutral in that educational funds are not tied to local property wealth. In these states, courts have emphasized that education is ultimately a state responsibility.

5. In a few states an adequate education has been judicially defined as one that fulfills the state constitutional obligation to provide a thorough and efficient or basic education for all students. These courts have required legislatures to identify and fully fund the components of an educational program that will meet the state's educational goals.

6. Some courts have held that the adequacy of private school programs should be assessed using outcome measures (i.e., student achievement data) rather than the input specifications (e.g., teacher qualifications, course prescriptions, etc.) that are commonly used to assess the sufficiency of public school programs. Other courts have upheld the state's authority to impose minimum program and personnel requirements on nonpublic schools to ensure an educated citizenry.

7. In general, courts have been more willing to interpret statutory directives than to create new constitutional law.

8. In cases involving special-need students, courts have been quite assertive in interpreting the statutory rights of these children and the accompanying obligations placed on education agencies to address their unique needs.

9. Courts have been unsympathetic when fiscal constraints have been offered as the rationale for not fulfilling statutory obligations.

### State Statutory and Regulatory Activity

1. Statutory enactments pertaining to education have become more detailed and broader in scope.

2. Most state education laws pertain to input requirements (e.g., teacher qualifications, school calendar, pupil/teacher ratio, prescribed courses, etc.), but the number of statutes pertaining to school accountability, student competency requirements, and the rights of special-need students has increased

in recent years.

3. Despite the proliferation of state laws, few state legislatures have attempted to identify the specific components of an adequate education for the general school population.

4. The most detailed standards of educational adequacy are found in state board of education regulations. The input requirements contained in school approval or accreditation schemes substitute for definitions of educational adequacy in most states.

5. Many state-imposed program standards are not reflected in state school support schemes, and the relationship between some input specifications and the attainment of educational outcomes is not well documented.

6. Efforts to improve the efficiency of schools through accountability mandates have been hampered by ill-defined educational goals.

7. Recent efforts to define an adequate education in terms of school outputs primarily have entailed the identification of minimum student competencies. The limits of psychometric knowledge, coupled with the lack of consensus as to desired outcomes of schooling, have resulted in a narrow focus for most minimum competency programs (mainly reading and computation skills).

8. With the exception of limited provisions for remedial programs, most state school support systems do not reflect school output standards.

9. In many states efforts to establish input and output specifications for schools are not sufficiently coordinated.

### Federal Role

1. The federal role in defining and establishing standards of educational adequacy mainly has involved targeted curricular areas and categories of pupils.

2. Through civil rights legislation and regulations and court decisions interpreting these mandates, education agencies have been required to provide specific services and programs to overcome past disadvantages or present disabilities of students.

3. Regulations attached to federal categorical aid programs and federal research, development, and dissemination activities also have influenced definitions and standards of educational adequacy.

4. The most specific federal pronouncements on the components of an adequate education have pertained to programs and services that must be provided for handicapped children.

5. Federal mandates have nurtured a double standard in assessing educational adequacy, in that the general educational program is usually considered adequate if it satisfies minimum state input requirements, whereas programs for special-need students must be appropriate to address the students' unique characteristics.

6. Targeted federal educational priorities (e.g., special education, compensatory education, vocational education) are reflected in most state school support schemes.

7. There are recent indications that the federal government intends to reduce or at least refocus its role in determining public educational policies and practices.

# Obstacles to Defining and Establishing Standards of Educational Adequacy

Most legal activity pertaining to educational adequacy is relatively recent, and such activity understandably lacks sufficient coordination at this time. Many unresolved issues have been noted in the preceding chapters. A couple of these issues pose particular barriers to efforts to define and assure educational adequacy for all students.

### Lack of Consensus Regarding Adequacy for What and for Whom

The term "adequacy," by definition, means sufficiency *for a given purpose.* Thus the adequacy of educational programs or school support systems cannot be assessed accurately until there is some agreement regarding *for what* the programs and resources must be sufficient. The purposes currently ascribed to public education are often ambiguous or all-encompassing. Global goal statements that schools should prepare students for adult roles or maximize their potential provide little guidance with respect to the specific components of the educational program that should be assured to all children.

By couching educational goals in global language, some controversial issues can be avoided. Should individual or societal, equity or liberty interests prevail? Should professionals play a major role in determining educational priorities, or should such decisions be left solely to political determination? Should educational purposes be prescribed at the state level or determined locally on the basis of local preferences and needs? Until these and other difficult questions are addressed, it seems likely that educational goals will continue to be phrased in language intended to satisfy everyone, thereby promising far more than schools reasonably can be expected to deliver.

It is not uncommon for a state's educational goals to assure equal educational opportunities, adequate instruction to prepare all children for citizenship and competition in a free enterprise economy, a range of educational offerings to produce well-rounded adults, and instruction tailored to the needs of each individual child. It is difficult at best to translate such all-encompassing goals into specific instructional programs and services. For example, what skills are necessary for an individual to compete successfully in the labor market? What level of competition is considered sufficient, and for what marketplace must one be prepared?

Without concrete goals to provide the foundation for definitions and standards of educational adequacy, school priorities are being determined by local, state, and federal input and output requirements that are imposed on schools. Some of these requirements seem to be grounded in conflicting notions about the purposes of public education. Additional responsibilities are being placed on schools by different levels of government without a consensus that public schools *can* (or should) assume these responsibilities. Public schools cannot solve all of society's problems. Realistic purposes for public education need to be identified so that resources can be concentrated on finding the most appropriate means to attain them.

When they identify goals and objectives for public schools, policy makers must also decide *for whom* instructional programs should be adequate. At present the standards to assess program adequacy vary according to the students being served. For normal-range students, the educational program is considered adequate if it satisfies minimum input requirements, but the program for certain pupils must be tailored to meet their unique needs. Sensitive issues must be addressed regarding the scope of the school's responsibility to meet the entire continuum of pupils' needs. Should a substantial portion of limited educational resources be expended to toilet train students or to provide catheterization and psychotherapy services? Should gifted as well as handicapped students be entitled to a publicly supported private education if the public school is not meeting their needs? Should public schools be responsible for preschool and adult education programs? Are schools attempting to perform some functions that could be handled more effectively by other public agencies? Without answers to these and similar questions, the components of the instructional program and standards of educational adequacy may be determined in part by the strength of lobbying efforts.

An apparent paradox must be resolved: Legislatures have been reluctant to establish concrete goals and objectives for schools, but at the same time input and output requirements have been established at an escalating rate. In essence, educational adequacy has been defined by the standards imposed, even though such standards may be based on faulty assumptions regarding for what and for whom educational programs should be adequate. Solutions have been implemented without thorough exploration of the problems they are designed to solve or the outcomes they are intended to achieve.[2] Until the incongruities between means and ends are addressed, the proliferation of legal mandates establishing educational input and output standards will not assure that educational programs are indeed *sufficient* for a *given purpose*.

## Translation of Input and Output Requirements into Funding Schemes

In the absence of legislative specification of the components of an adequate education, minimum input standards usually serve as "proxies" for a definition of educational adequacy. It is assumed that schools are providing sufficient programs for normal-range students if such minimum criteria are satisfied. In general, input standards are promulgated by state boards of education and developed by state department personnel relying on the collective judgment of experts in the field or on data pertaining to past practices within the state. There is little documentation to show that many of the input standards currently imposed on schools are directly related to the attainment of specific outcomes. A program might be considered adequate on the basis of input standards, even though the envisioned outcomes of the program have not been attained (e.g., student mastery of basic skills).

While there is an escalating movement to develop output measures of educational adequacy, substantial controversy persists over what outcomes should be assessed. For example, should outcome standards be defined in terms of basic academic skills or on the basis of other criteria such as employment or income? Because of the difficulties associated with measuring the long-range outcomes of schooling, most output measures have been confined to student achievement in basic skill areas, primarily reading and mathematics. Even in this limited domain the establishment of student performance standards and statewide assessment programs has not been sufficiently coordinated with school accreditation or approval standards. Thus conflicting input and output specifications have been simultaneously imposed on some schools. For example, a given school may be required to devote a certain percentage of the instructional day to creative and applied arts, while the effectiveness of the school is being judged on the basis of whether students master minimum skills in reading and mathematics.

Other problems are associated with output standards of educational adequacy. The procedures used to assess pupil performance have been vulnerable to attack on both legal and educational grounds. Student testing programs continue to be plagued by questions pertaining to the curricular validity and racial and cultural bias of the instruments used. Also, data are not currently available to link student performance (in the narrow domain that is assessed) to specific programmatic features or pedagogical practices.

Moreover, the input and output specifications being imposed on schools are often not reflected in state school support systems. Most states do not assure *full* support of the educational program that must be provided to satisfy state regulations. In several states standards imposed upon schools by state boards of education have become more detailed without significant changes in educational funding schemes. In fact, in a few cases the percentage of school funds supplied at the state level has actually declined in recent years, although state-imposed requirements pertaining to program components have become more extensive.[3]

If all students are expected to master certain competencies before leaving public schools, provisions should be made for the students who will require remedial programs and perhaps additional years of schooling. Similarly, if the basic education program is expected to satisfy specific state-imposed standards, there must be assurances that sufficient funds are available for those standards to be met. Furthermore, if educational adequacy is to be assessed on the basis of whether schools are meeting the needs of each individual learner, more sophisticated systems of reflecting the costs associated with addressing various types of students' needs will have to be devised. Unless input and output requirements are directly reflected in school funding schemes, school districts may be faced with continually increasing demands and decreasing resources with which to meet those demands.

## Outlook for the 1980s

It seems likely that school finance reform efforts increasingly will focus on adequacy in addition to equity concerns. This change in emphasis can be attributed to a combination of factors. For example, as state legislatures have assumed a greater share of the fiscal responsibility for education, they have become more interested in the *substance* of educational offerings. Responding to court rulings, committee recommendations, and public demands for accountability, legislatures seem destined to become more active in defining the components of the *minimum education* that must be assured throughout the state.

Also, the federal government has given some indication that its educational priorities may be shifting from equity toward adequacy concerns. The Reagan administration has taken the position that school access and equity goals have been sufficiently addressed by state and local education agencies; therefore, burdensome federal regulations are no longer needed in this arena. While it appears unlikely that Congress will totally abandon its efforts to attain educational equity, there is some sentiment that the federal government will focus greater attention on providing incentives (and pressure) to improve educational outcomes in terms of pupil achievement.[4]

In addition, the notion of adequacy has more appeal than does equity to those interested in the preservation of local control. Wise has asserted that local schools "should be held responsible for the production of education, while other levels and branches of government should be held responsible for ensuring equity within schools. . . ."[5] Although equity issues require some degree of centralized policy intervention, there is mounting sentiment that local communities should not be disenfranchised in educational decision making. Thus, the inherent conflict between the concepts of liberty and equity has been brought into focus.[6] A commitment to make educational opportunities equitable among all school districts within a state often results in a reduction in discretionary powers of local school districts to provide educational offerings at a level of their own choosing. However, it is possible to mandate that an adequate education be provided throughout a state without equitable opportunities being required. Indeed, this is essentially the position assumed by the United States Supreme Court in *Rodriguez*.[7] The Court concluded that interdistrict disparities can be overlooked as long as the state ensures that all students receive a *minimum* education necessary for the exercise of constitutional rights and full participation in the democratic process.

The difference between the *Rodriguez* rationale and future judicial rulings seems likely to center on an interpretation of the "quantum" of education required. The *Rodriguez* majority assumed that the state's minimum foundation program supported the necessary basic educational program and that state accreditation standards provided assurances that all school districts were providing an adequate education. Such assumptions may not be accepted by future courts as readily as they have been in the past. Courts may be more inclined to require legislatures to specify the envisioned outcomes of schooling and to identify the components of the educational program necessary to attain those outcomes.

As legislatures become increasingly specific in prescribing the skills, behaviors, and knowledge that should be acquired by students, it seems inevitable that support systems will have to reflect school outputs as well as inputs. For example, provisions will need to be made for remedial instruction for students who do not demonstrate mastery of designated skills. Some states already require an individualized educational program to be developed for students with identified basic skill deficiencies.[8] The emphasis on outcomes may ultimately lead to more precise measures of student need.

An outcome orientation toward the state's obligation to provide an adequate education might also generate substantial litigation in which courts will be asked to evaluate whether particular programs are sufficient to assure student mastery of prescribed skills and whether these skills are sufficient for the state's educational goals to be attained (e.g., to prepare students for employment). If legislatures promise more than can be delivered, school districts may become vulnerable to instructional negligence suits. This type of litigation might bring into focus the need for additional research documenting what skills (school outputs) are needed for success in various life roles (school outcomes) and what instructional resources are necessary to teach the skills identified.

Research currently available in this arena is deficient in both focus and rigor; findings often are nonconfirmatory or contradictory. For example, teaching experience and advanced degrees are major determinants of teachers' salaries, but these variables are not clearly related to improvements in school outputs.[9] Perhaps a "second generation" of production function studies will provide a reliable body of information, isolating the impact of changes in resources on changes in school effects.[10]

Such information is needed to safeguard education from substantial budget cuts as public funds shrink. Education has not been able to provide cost/benefit data as readily as have some other public services, and the citizenry appears less sanguine about the efficacy of public schools than was true in the past.[11] In 1981 the Education Commission of the States reported that nearly two-thirds of the states face critical shortages in educational funds, resulting from a combination of inflation, the general state of the economy, tax limitation measures, and efforts to trim governmental spending.[12]

The legal activity to define and establish standards of educational adequacy possibly will result in realistic and concrete educational goals and research relating programs and resources to the attainment of those goals. Legislative committees in several states such as Montana and South Dakota are currently attempting to define the components of an adequate education.[13] As additional states identify such program features and guarantee their full support, perhaps the rhetoric of educational adequacy will become a reality.

---

1. Cynthia Ward, "School Finance Project Opinion Survey," *Journal of Education Finance* 6, no. 4 (1981):505-11.

2. Martha McCarthy, "Adequacy in Educational Programs: A Legal Perspective," in *Perspectives in State School Support Systems*, ed. K. F. Jordan and Nelda Cambron, (Cambridge, Mass.: Ballinger Pub. Co. 1981).

3. In Virginia, for example, the state-mandated standards of quality have become more elaborate but the portion of educational revenues supplied by the state has decreased. See Richard Salmon and Ralph Shotwell, "Virginia School Finance Reform: Status Quo Maintained," *Journal of Education Finance* 3, no. 4 (1978):527.

4. *See* David Clark and Mary Anne Amiot, "The Impact of the Reagan Administration on Federal Education Policy," *Phi Delta Kappan* 63, no. 4 (1981):258-59.

5. Arthur Wise, *Legislated Learning* (Berkeley, Calif.: University of California Press, 1979), p. 203.

6. *See* Norman Thomas, "Equalizing Educational Opportunity Through School Finance Reform: A Review Assessment," *University of Cincinnati Law Review* 48 (1979):267.

7. 411 U.S. 1 (1973).

8. In New Jersey, for example, students with identified basic-skill deficiencies in sixth grade must be provided an Individualized Student Improvement Plan (ISIP). *See* Fred G. Burke, *Guidelines for High School Graduation Requirements* (Trenton, N.J.: New Jersey State Department of Education, 1980), p. 5; *See* chapter 4, text with note 68.

9. Harvey Averch, Stephen Carroll, Theodore Donaldson, Herbert Kiesling, and John Pincus, *How Effective is Schooling? A Critical Review and Synthesis of Research Findings* (Santa Monica, Calif.: The Rand Corporation, 1972), p. 155.

10. *See* Frederick Sebold and William Dato, "School Funding and Student Achievement: An Empirical Analysis," *Public Finance Quarterly* 9, no. 1 (1981):91-105; Charles Benson, *The Economics of Public Education* (Boston, Mass.: Houghton Mifflin Co., 1978), pp. 201-3.

11. *See* Clark and Amiot, "The Impact of the Reagan Administration on Federal Education Policy," p. 259.

12. *States in a Squeeze: Major Education Challenges of the Early '80s* (Denver, Colo.: Education Commission of the States, 1981).

13. Interviews with Sandra Kissick, Director of the Education Program, National Conference of State Legislatures, Washington, D.C., and Charles Cheney, Legislative Consultant, University of North Dakota, Grand Forks, North Dakota.

# Appendix A

## Selected Cases Pertaining to Educational Adequacy in Public School Programs*

### School Finance Cases

**State Support Schemes**

Alma School Dist. v. Dupree, No. 77-406 (Ark. Chancery, Pulaski County, 1981).

Board of Educ., Levittown Union Free School Dist., Nassau County v. Nyquist, 408 N.Y.S. 2d 606 (Sup. Ct., Nassau County, 1978), *aff'd as modified*, 443 N.Y.S.2d 843 (App. Div. 1981).

Boston Teachers Union v. City of Boston, 416 N.E.2d 1363 (Mass. 1981).

Department of Educ. v. School Bd. of Collier County, 394 So. 2d 1010 (Fla. 1981).

Thomas v. Stewart, No. 8275 (Ga. Super., Polk County, 1981), *rev'd*, McDaniel v. Thomas, 285 S.E.2d 156 (Ga. 1981).

Board of Educ. of the City School Dist. of the City of Cincinnati v. Walter, 390 N.E.2d 812 (Ohio 1979), *cert. denied*, 444 U.S. 1015 (1980).

*In re* Board of Educ. of the City of Trenton, 424 A.2d 435 (N.J. 1980).

Washakie County School District No. 1 v. Herschler, 606 P.2d 310 (Wyo. 1980), *cert. denied sub nom.* Hot Springs County School Dist. No. 1 v. Washakie County School Dist. No. 1, 499 U.S. 842 (1980).

Board of Educ. of Township High School Dist. No. 206 v. Cronin, 388 N.E.2d 72 (Ill. App. 1979).

Centennial School Dist. v. Commonwealth Dep't of Educ., 408 A.2d 211 (Pa. Commw. 1979).

---

*Cases are cited in reverse chronological order under each section.

Danson v. Casey, 399 A.2d 360 (Pa. 1979).

Karcher v. Byrne, 399 A.2d 644 (N.J. 1979).

Lujan v. State Bd. of Educ., No. 79 SA 276 (D. Colo. 1979).

Newcome v. Board of Educ. of Tucker City, 260 S.E.2d 462 (W. Va. App. 1979).

O'Donnell v. Casey, 405 A.2d 1006 (Pa. Commw. 1979).

Pauley v. Kelly, 255 S.E.2d 859 (W. Va. 1979).

Somerset County Bd. of Educ. v. Hornbeck (Md. Cir. Ct., Baltimore City, 1979), reported in *Education Daily*, 21 May 1981, pp. 1-2.

State *ex rel.* Conger v. Madison County, 581 S.W.2d 632 (Tenn. 1979).

Board of Educ. v. Walter, 10 Ohio Op. 3d 26 (Ohio App. 1978).

Horne v. Louisiana State Bd. of Educ., 357 So. 2d 1216 (La. App. 1978), *writ denied*, 359 So. 2d 621 (La. 1978).

Seattle School Dist. No. 1 of King County v. Washington, 585 P.2d 71 (Wash. 1978).

Township of Princeton v. New Jersey Dep't. of Educ., 394 A.2d 1240 (N.J. Super. App. Div. 1978).

Board of Educ. v. Superintendent of Public Instr., 257 N.W.2d 73 (Mich. 1977).

Board of Educ. v. Walter, No. A760275 (Ohio C.P., Hamilton County, 1977).

Oster v. Kneip, No. 77-365 (S.D. Cir. Ct., Hughes County, filed 1977).

Wehde v. Erickson, No. 77-652 (S.D. Cir. Ct., Minnehaha County, filed 1977).

Knowles v. State Bd. of Educ., 547 P.2d 699 (Kan. 1976).

Matter of Levy, 382 N.Y.S.2d 13 (N.Y. 1976).

Olsen v. State of Oregon, 554 P.2d 139 (Or. 1976).

People of the State of Illinois *ex rel.* Jones v. Adams, 40 Ill. App. 3d 189 (1976).

Robinson VI, 358 A.2d 457 (N.J. 1976).

Robinson V, 355 A.3d 129 (N.J. 1976).

Scarnato v. Parker, 415 F. Supp. 272 (M.D. La. 1976).

Serrano v. Priest, 557 P.2d 929 (Cal. 1976) "Serrano II."

Boothbay v. Langley, No. 75-918 (Me. Super., Kennebec County, 1975) (dismissed as moot).

Northwestern School Dist. v. Pittenger, 397 F. Supp. 975 (W.D. Pa. 1975).

Robinson IV, 351 A.2d 713 (N.J. 1975).

Robinson III, 339 A.2d 193 (N.J. 1975).

Thompson v. Engelking, 537 P.2d 635 (Idaho 1975).

Horton v. Meskill, 332 A.2d 113 (Conn. 1974).

Northshore School Dist. No. 417 v. Kinnear, 530 P.2d 178 (Wash. 1974).

Woodahl v. Straub, 520 P.2d 776 (Mont. 1974), *cert. denied,* 419 U.S. 845 (1974).

Blase v. State, 302 N.E.2d 46 (Ill. 1973).

Robinson II, 306 A.2d 65 (N.J. 1973).

Robinson v. Cahill, 287 A.2d 187 (N.J. Super. 1972), *aff'd as modified,* 303 A.2d 273 (N.J. 1973) "Robinson I."

San Antonio Independent School Dist. v. Rodriguez, 411 U.S. 1 (1973).

Shofstall v. Hollins, 515 P.2d 590 (Ariz. 1973).

State *ex rel.* Brotherton v. Blankenship, 207 S.E.2d 421 (W. Va. 1973).

Caldwell v. Kansas, No. 50616 (D. Kan. 1972).

Milliken v. Green, 203 N.W.2d 457 (Mich. 1972).

Parker v. Mandel, 344 F. Supp. 1068 (D. Md. 1972).

Serrano v. Priest, 487 P.2d 1241 (Cal. 1971) "Serrano I."

Van Dusartz v. Hatfield, 334 F. Supp. 870 (D. Minn. 1971).

Board of Educ. of Elizabeth v. City Council, 262 A. 2d 881 (N.J. 1970).

Burruss v. Wilkerson, 310 F. Supp. 572 (W.D. Va. 1969), *aff'd mem.,* 397 U.S. 44 (1970).

Hargrave v. Kirk, 313 F. Supp. 944 (M.D. Fla. 1970), *vacated on other grounds sub nom.* Askew v. Hargrave, 401 U.S. 476 (1971).

McInnis v. Shapiro, 293 F. Supp. 327 (N.D. Ill. 1968), *aff'd mem. sub nom.* McInnis v. Ogilvie, 394 U.S. 322 (1969).

LeBeauf v. State Bd. of Educ., 244 F. Supp. 256 (E.D. La. 1965).

People v. Deatherage, 81 N.E.2d 581 (Ill. 1948).

Louisville v. Board of Educ., 195 S.W.2d 291 (Ky. 1946).

Commonwealth *ex rel.* Baxter v. Burnett, 35 S.W.2d 857 (Ky. 1931).

Board of Educ. v. McChesney, 32 S.W.2d 26 (Ky. 1930).

State *ex rel.* King v. Sherman, 135 N.E.2d 625 (Ohio 1922).

Dickinson v. Edmondson, 178 S.W. 930 (Ark. 1915).

**Taxation**

Polick v. Chicago School Finance Authority, 402 N.E.2d 247 (Ill. 1980).

School Dist. No. 25, Bannock County v. State Tax Comm'n, 612 P.2d 126 (Idaho 1980).

Inhabitants of Town of Stonington v. Inhabitants of Town of Deer Isle, 403 A.2d 1181 (Me. 1979).

Paul L. Smith, Inc. v. Southern York County School Dist., 403 A.2d 1034 (Pa. Commw. 1979).

Thompson v. Anding, 370 So. 2d 1335 (Miss. 1979).

Amador Valley Joint Union High School Dist. v. State Bd. of Equalization, 149 Cal. Rptr. 239 (Cal. 1978).

Citizens for Fair Taxes v. Brockette, No. A-77-CA-106 (W.D. Tex. 1978).

Swanton Local School Dist. Library v. Budget Comm'n of Lucas County, 378 N.E.2d 139 (Ohio 1978).

Tooley v. O'Connell, 253 N.W.2d 335 (Wis. 1977).

Buse v. Smith, 247 N.W.2d 141 (Wis. 1976).

Dornacker v. Olson, 248 N.W.2d 844 (N.D. 1976).

Harte v. Lehnhausen, 328 N.E.2d 543 (Ill. 1975), *cert. denied,* 423 U.S. 912 (1976).

Lafayette Steel Company v. City of Dearborn, 360 F. Supp. 1127 (E.D. Mich. 1973).

Board of Educ. of Louisville v. Board of Educ. of Jefferson County, 458 S.W.2d 6 (Ky. 1970).

Rainwater v. Haynes, 428 S.W.2d 254 (Ark. 1968).

Pingry Corporation v. Township of Hillside, 217 A.2d 868 (N.J. 1966).

Brennan v. Black, 104 A.2d 777 (Del. 1954).

State *ex rel.* Bd. of Educ. of City of Minneapolis v. Erickson, 251 N.W.519 (Minn. 1933).

Board of Supervisors of King and Queen County v. Cox, 156 S.E. 755 (Va. 1931).

McNair v. School Dist. No. 1, 288 P. 188 (Mont. 1930).

Fiedler v. Eckfeldt, 166 N.E. 504 (Ill. 1929).

Moseley v. City of Dallas, 17 S.W.2d 36 (Tex. App. 1929).

Richardson v. Liberty Independent School Dist., 22 S.W.2d 475 (Tex. Civ. App. 1929).

Miller v. Korns, 140 N.E. 773 (Ohio 1923).

*In re* School Code of 1919, 108 A. 39 (Del. 1919).

Society for Establishing Useful Manufactures v. City of Paterson, 98 A. 440 (N.J. 1916).

Associated Schools of Independent Dist. No. 63 v. School Dist. No. 83, 142 N.W. 325 (Minn. 1913).

Fenton v. Board of Comm'rs of Ada County, 119 P. 41 (Idaho 1911).

McIntire v. Powell, 125 S.W. 1087 (Ky. 1910).

City of Louisville v. Commonwealth, 121 S.W. 411 (Ky. 1909).

Evers v. Hudson, 92 P. 462 (Mont. 1907).

Revell v. Annapolis, 31 A. 695 (Md. 1895).


**Fees for Textbooks and Courses**

Doe v. Plyer, 628 F.2d 448 (5th Cir. 1980), *cert. granted,* 101 S. Ct. 2044 (1981).

Board of Educ. of Freeport Union Free School Dist. v. Nyquist, 430 N.Y.S.2d 266 (N.Y. 1980).

Sneed v. Greensboro City Bd. of Educ., 264 S.E.2d 106 (N.C. 1980).

Crim v. McWhorter, 252 S.E.2d 421 (Ga. 1979).

Foster v. County School Bd. of Prince William County, 48 U.S.L.W. 3128 (Va. 1979), *cert. denied,* 444 U.S. 804 (1980).

Cardiff v. Bismark Public School Dist., 263 N.W.2d 105 (N.D. 1978).

Chapp v. High School Dist. No. 1 of Pima County, 574 P.2d 493 (Ariz. App. 1978).

Sodus Central School v. Rhine, 406 N.Y.S.2d 175 (App. Div. 1978).

Concerned Parents v. Caruthersville School Dist., 548 S.W.2d 554 (Mo. 1977).

Beck v. Board of Educ. of Harlem Consolidated School Dist., 344 N.E.2d 440 (Ill. 1976).

Marshall v. School Dist. Re No. 3 Morgan County, 553 P.2d 784 (Colo. 1976).

Norton v. Board of Educ. of School Dist. No. 16, Hobbs Municipal Schools, 553 P.2d 1277 (N.M. 1976).

Carpio v. Tucson High School Dist. No. 1 of Pima County, 524 P. 2d 948 (Ariz. 1974).

Chandler v. South Bend Community School Corp., 312 N.E.2d 915 (Ind. App. 1974).

Vandevender v. Cassell, 208 S.E.2d 436 (W. Va. 1974).

Granger v. Cascade County School Dist., 499 P.2d 780 (Mont. 1972).

Johnson v. New York State Educ. Dep't, 449 F.2d 871 (2d Cir. 1971), *vacated and remanded*, 409 U.S. 75 (1972) (per curiam).

# Scope of Legislative Authority Regarding Provision of Education

Bryne v. Alexander, 425 A.2d 602 (Pa. Commw. 1981).

Corliss v. Soloman, 427 N.Y.S.2d 868 (App. Div. 1980).

Deriso v. Cooper, 272 S.E.2d 274 (Ga. 1980).

Saline County Bd. of Educ. v. Hot Spring County Bd. of Educ., 603 S.W.2d 413 (Ark. 1980).

Walker v. Board of Educ. of Olean City School Dist., 433 N.Y.S.2d 660 (App. Div. 1980).

Blumer v. School Bd. of Beresford Independent School Dist., 250 N.W.2d 282 (S.D. 1977).

Cronin v. Lindberg, 360 N.E.2d 360 (Ill. 1977).

Hootch v. Alaska State-Operated School System, 536 P.2d 793 (Alaska 1975).

Jeter v. Ellenville Central School Dist., 377 N.Y.S.2d 685 (App. Div. 1975).

Morris v. Board of Educ. of Laurel School Dist., 401 F. Supp. 188 (D. Del. 1975).

Corder v. City of Milford, 196 A.2d 406 (Del. Super., Sussex County, 1963).

Howard v. County School Board of Allegheny County, 122 S.E.2d 891 (Va. 1961).

Harrison v. Day, 106 S.E.2d 636 (Va. 1959).

Wooley v. Spalding, 293 S.W.2d 563 (Ky. 1956).

State ex rel. Trent v. Sims, 77 S.E.2d 122 (W. Va. 1953).

Board of Supervisors of Chesterfield County v. County School Bd. of Chesterfield County, 28 S.E.2d 698 (Va. 1944).

American Nat. Bank of Idaho Falls v. Joint Independent School Dist. No. 9, 102 P.2d 826 (Idaho 1940).

Ehret v. School Dist. of Kulpmont, 5 A.2d 188 (Pa. 1939).

Commonwealth ex rel. Meredith v. Norfleet, 115 S.W.2d 353 (Ky. 1938).

Malone v. Hayden, 197 A. 344 (Pa. 1938).

State ex rel. Lien v. School Dist. No. 73, 76 P.2d 330 (Mont. 1938).

Grant v. Michaels, 23 P.2d 266 (Mont. 1933).

Board of Educ. of City of Minneapolis v. Houghton, 233 N.W. 834 (Minn. 1930).

Manley v. Moon, 6 S.W.2d 281 (Ark. 1928).

Flory v. Smith, 134 S.E. 360 (Va. 1926).

Board of Educ. v. Moorehead, 136 N.W. 913 (Ohio 1922).

People ex rel. Russell v. Graham, 134 N.E. 57 (Ill. 1922).

State ex rel. Methodist Children's Home v. Board of Educ., 138 N.E. 865 (Ohio 1922).

Houston v. Gonzales Independent School Dist., 202 S.W. 963 (Tex. Civ. App. 1918).

Herold v. McQueen, 75 S.E. 313 (W. Va. 1912).

Florman v. School Dist. No. 11, 40 P. 469 (1895).

*In re* Kindergarten Schools, 32 P. 422 (Colo. 1893).

Kuhn v. Board of Educ. of Wellsburg, 4 W. Va. 499 (1871).

## Compulsory Attendance/Equivalent Instruction

State of Nebraska v. Faith Baptist Church, 301 N.W.2d 471 (Neb. 1981), *appeal dismissed sub nom.* Faith Baptist Church v. Douglas, 102 S. Ct. 75 (1981).

State of West Virginia v. Riddle, 285 S.E.2d 359 (W. Va. 1981).

Committee for Public Educ. and Religious Liberty v. Regan, 444 U.S. 948 (1980).

Hanson v. Cushman, 490 F. Supp. 109 (W.D. Mich. 1980).

Kentucky State Bd. for Elementary and Secondary Educ. v. Rudasill, 589 S.W.2d 877 (Ky. 1979), *cert. denied,* 446 U.S. 938 (1980).

McKeesport Area School Dist. v. Pennsylvania Dep't of Educ., 446 U.S. 970 (1980).

State v. Shaver, 294 N.W.2d 883 (N.D. 1980).

State *ex rel.* Nagle v. Olin, 415 N.E.2d 281 (Ohio 1980).

State Fire Marshall v. Lee, 300 N.W.2d 748 (Mich. App. 1980).

Wells v. Banks, 266 S.E.2d 270 (Ga. App. 1980).

City of Akron v. Lane, 416 N.E.2d 642 (Ohio App. 1979).

Hill v. State, 381 So. 2d 91 (Ala. App. 1979).

In Interest of Rice, 285 N.W. 2d 223 (Neb. 1979).

State v. Vietto, 252 S.E.2d 732 (N.C. 1979).

State of Missouri v. Davis, 598 S.W.2d 189 (Mo. App. 1979).

Cleary v. Lash, 401 N.Y.S.2d 124 (Nassau County Ct. 1977).

In the Matter of Franz, 390 N.Y.S.2d 940 (App. Div. 1977).

Wolman v. Walters, 433 U.S. 229 (1977).

*In re* Gregory B., 387 N.Y.S.2d 380 (Fam. Ct. 1976).

*In re* McMillan, 226 S.E.2d 693 (N.C. App. 1976).

State v. LaBarge, 357 A.2d 121 (Vt. 1976).

State of Ohio v. Whisner, 351 N.E.2d 750 (Ohio 1976).

*In re* Eric and Liisa Davis, 318 A.2d 151 (N.H. 1974).

*In re* Thomas H., 357 N.Y.S.2d 384 (Fam. Ct. 1974).

Scoma v. The Chicago Bd. of Educ., 391 F. Supp. 452 (N.D. Ill. 1974).

F. & F. v. Duval County, 273 So. 2d 15 (Fla. Dist. Ct. App. 1973).

Wisconsin v. Yoder, 406 U.S. 205 (1972).

Zebra v. School Dist. of City of Pittsburgh, 296 A.2d 748 (Pa. 1972).

Lemon v. Kurtzman, 403 U.S. 602 (1971).

Board of Educ. v. Allen, 392 U.S. 236 (1968).

State v. Garber, 419 P.2d 896 (Kan. 1966), *cert. denied,* 389 U.S. 51 (1967).

State of New Jersey v. Massa, 231 A.2d 252 (Morris County Ct. 1967).

City of Chicopee v. Jakubowski, 202 N.E.2d 913 (Mass. 1964).

State v. Lowry, 383 P.2d 962 (Kan. 1963).

Board of Educ. of Aberdeen-Huntington Local School Dist. v. State Bd. of Educ., 189 N.E.2d 81 (Ohio App. 1962).

*In re* Shinn, 16 Cal. Rptr. 165 (Dist. Ct. App. 1961).

Shoreline School Dist. v. Superior Court for King County, 346 P.2d 999 (Wash. 1959), *cert. denied,* 363 U.S. 814 (1960).

State v. Pilkinton, 310 S.W.2d 304 (Mo. App. 1958).

Sheppard v. State, 306 P.2d 346 (Okla. Crim. App. 1957).

Commonwealth v. Renfrew, 126 N.E.2d 109 (Mass. 1955).

People v. Turner, 236 P.2d 685 (Cal. App. Dep't Super. Ct. 1953), *appeal dismissed,* 347 U.S. 972 (1953).

Knox v. O'Brien, 72 A.2d 389 (N.J. Cape May County Ct. 1950).

People v. Levisen, 90 N.E.2d 213 (Ill. 1950).

People v. Turner, 98 N.Y.S.2d 886 (App. Div. 1950).

Rice v. Commonwealth, 49 S.E.2d 342 (Va. 1948).

Prince v. Massachusetts, 321 U.S. 158 (1944).

West Virginia Bd. of Educ. v. Barnette, 319 U.S. 624 (1943).

Stephens v. Bongart, 189 A. 131 (N.J. Essex County Ct. 1937).

Vollmar v. Stanley, 255 P. 610 (Colo. 1927).

Pierce v. Society of Sisters, 268 U.S. 510 (1925).

Meyer v. Nebraska, 262 U.S. 390 (1923).

St. John's Military Academy v. Edwards, 128 N.W. 113 (Wis. 1910).

State v. Peterman, 70 N.E. 550 (Ind. App. 1904).

State v. Bailey, 61 N.E. 730 (Ind. 1901).

Commonwealth v. Roberts, 34 N.E. 402 (Mass. 1893).

# Rights of Handicapped Students

### Right to School Access and to Appropriate Programs

Springdale School Dist. v. Grace, 494 F. Supp. 266 (W.D. Ark. 1980), *aff'd,* 656 F.2d 300 (8th Cir. 1981).

Age v. Bullitt County Public Schools, 3 EHLR 551:505 (W.D. Ky. 1980).

DeWalt v. Burkholder, 3 EHLR 551:550 (E.D. Va. 1980).

In the Matter of Charles Hartman, 409 N.E.2d 1211 (Ind. App. 1980).

Matter of Gano, 432 N.Y.S.2d 764 (Fam. Ct. 1980).

New Mexico Ass'n for Retarded Citizens v. New Mexico, No. 75-633-M (D.N.M. 1980).

Plitt v. Madden, 413 A.2d 867 (Del. 1980).

Robert M. v. Benton, 634 F.2d 1139 (8th Cir. 1980).

Rowley v. Board of Educ. of the Hendrick Hudson School Dist., 483 F. Supp. 528 (S.D.N.Y. 1980), *aff'd,* 632 F.2d 945 (2d Cir. 1980).

Sessions v. Livingston Parish School Bd., 501 F. Supp. 251 (M.D. La. 1980).

Tatro v. State of Texas, 481 F. Supp. 1224 (N.D. Tex. 1979), *vacated and remanded,* 625 F.2d 557 (5th Cir. 1980).

Boxall v. Sequoia Union High School Dist., 464 F. Supp. 1104 (N.D. Cal. 1979).

Krawitz v. Commonwealth of Pennsylvania, 408 A.2d 1202 (Pa. Commw. 1979).

Mattie T. v. Holladay, No. DC-75-31s (N.D. Miss. 1979).

New York Ass'n for Retarded Children v. Carey, 466 F. Supp. 487 (E.D. N.Y. 1979).

O'Grady v. Centennial School Dist., 401 A.2d 1388 (Pa. Commw. 1979).

West Chester Area School Dist. v. Commonwealth Secretary of Educ., 410 A.2d 610 (Pa. Commw. 1979).

Lora v. Board of Educ. of the City of New York, 456 F. Supp. 1211 (E.D. N.Y. 1978).

Sherer v. Waier, 457 F. Supp. 1039 (W.D. Mo. 1978).

Frederick L. v. Thomas, 419 F. Supp. 960 (E.D. Pa. 1976), *aff'd,* 557 F.2d 373 (3d Cir. 1977).

Kampmeier v. Nyquist, 553 F.2d 296 (2d Cir. 1977).

Panitch v. State of Wisconsin, 444 F. Supp. 320 (E.D. Wis. 1977).

State v. Stecher, 390 A.2d 408 (Conn. Super. 1977).

Cuyahoga County Ass'n for Retarded Children and Adults v. Essex, 411 F. Supp. 46 (N.D. Ohio 1976).

Hairston v. Drosick, 423 F. Supp. 180 (S.D. W. Va. 1976).

*In re* Loft, 383 N.Y.S.2d 142 (Fam. Ct. 1976).

Denver Ass'n of Retarded Children, Inc. v. School Dist. No. 1 of Denver, 535 P.2d 200 (Colo. 1975).

Fialkowski v. Shapp, 405 F. Supp. 946 (E.D. Pa. 1975).

In the Matter of John Young, 377 N.Y.S.2d 429 (Fam. Ct. 1975).

*In re* G. H., 218 N.W.2d 441 (N.D. 1974).

Maryland Ass'n for Retarded Children v. State, No. 100-182-77676 (Md. Cir. Ct., Baltimore County, April 6, 1974).

New York State Ass'n for Retarded Children v. Rockefeller, 357 F. Supp. 752 (E.D.N.Y. 1973).

Mills v. Board of Educ., 348 F. Supp. 866 (D.D.C. 1972).

Pennsylvania Ass'n for Retarded Children v. Commonwealth, 343 F. Supp. 279 (E.D. Pa. 1972).

**Right to Private Placements**

Board of Educ. of Manchester v. Connecticut State Bd. of Educ., 427 A.2d 846 (Conn. 1981).

Gladys J. v. Pearland Independent School Dist., 520 F. Supp. 869 (S.D. Tex. 1981).

Kruelle v. Biggs, 489 F. Supp. 169 (D. Del. 1980), *aff'd sub nom.*
Kruelle v. New Castle County School Dist., 642 F.2d 687 (3d Cir.
1981).

Erdman v. State of Connecticut, 3 EHLR 552:218 (D. Conn. 1980).

Gary B. v. Cronin, 3 EHLR 551:633 (N.D. Ill. 1980).

Guemple v. State of New Jersey, 387 A.2d 399 (N.J. Super. 1978),
*modified,* 418 A.2d 229 (N.J. 1980).

Hines v. Pitt City Bd. of Educ., 497 F. Supp. 403 (E.D. N.C. 1980).

Lafko v. Wappingers Central School Dist., 427 N.Y.S.2d 529 (App.
Div. 1980).

Organization to Assure Services for Exceptional Students v. Amback,
432 N.Y.S.2d 54 (Sup. Ct., Albany County, 1980).

School Committee Town of Truro v. Commonwealth of Massachusetts,
3 EHLR 552:186 (Mass. Super. 1980).

Smith v. Cumberland School Committee, 415 A.2d 168 (R.I. 1980).

Ashbourne School v. Commonwealth Dep't of Educ., 403 A.2d 161 (Pa.
Commw. 1979).

Doe v. Grile, 3 EHLR 551:285 (N.D. Ind. 1979).

Grymes v. Madden, 3 EHLR 552:183 (D. Del. 1979).

Ladson v. Board of Educ., 3 EHLR 551:188 (D.D.C. 1979).

Matter of "A" Family, 602 P.2d 157 (Mont. 1979).

Matthews v. Campbell, 3 EHLR 551:265 (E.D. Va. 1979).

Michael P. v. Maloney, 3 EHLR 551:155 (D. Conn. 1979).

Moran v. Board of Directors of School Dist. of Kansas City, 584 S.W.2d
154 (Mo. App. 1979).

North v. District of Columbia Bd. of Educ., 471 F. Supp. 136 (D.D.C.
1979).

Stemple v. Board of Educ. of Prince George's County, 464 F. Supp. 258
(D. Md. 1979).

Welsch v. Commonwealth of Pennsylvania, 400 A.2d 234 (Pa. Commw.
1979).

William C. v. Board of Educ. of City of Chicago, 390 N.E.2d 479 (Ill.
App. 1979).

Elliot v. Board of Educ. of City of Chicago, 380 N.E.2d 1137 (Ill. App. 1978).

Scavella v. School Bd. of Dade County, 363 So. 2d 1095 (Fla. 1978).

Lux v. Connecticut State Bd. of Educ., 386 A.2d 644 (Conn. C.P., Fairfield County, 1977).

Meyer v. City of New York, 392 N.Y.S.2d 468 (App. Div. 1977).

In the Matter of Saberg, 386 N.Y.S.2d 592 (Fam. Ct. 1976).

In the Matter of Suzanne, 381 N.Y.S.2d 628 (Fam. Ct. 1976).

**Right to Year-Round Programs**

Armstrong v. Kline, 476 F. Supp. 583 (E.D. Pa. 1979), *aff'd*, 629 F.2d 269 (3d Cir. 1980), *cert. denied sub nom.* Scanlon v. Battle, 101 S. Ct. 3123 (1981).

Georgia Ass'n of Retarded Citizens v. McDaniel, 511 F. Supp. 1263 (N.D. Ga. 1981).

Anderson v. Thompson, 3 EHLR 552:251 (E.D. Wis. 1980).

In the Matter of Frank G., 414 N.Y.S.2d 851 (Fam. Ct. 1979).

In the Matter of George Jones, 414 N.Y.S.2d 258 (Fam. Ct. 1979).

Mahoney v. Administrative School Dist. No. 1, 601 P.2d 826 (Ore. App. 1979).

In the Matter of Scott K., 400 N.Y.S.2d 289 (Fam. Ct. 1977).

Schneps v. Nyquist, 396 N.Y.S.2d 275 (App. Div. 1977).

In the Matter of Richard G., 383 N.Y.S.2d 403 (App. Div. 1976).

In the Matter of Stein, 365 N.Y.S.2d 450 (Fam. Ct. 1975).

**Application of Disciplinary Procedures**

S-1 v. Turlington, 635 F.2d 342 (5th Cir. 1981), *cert. denied*, 102 S. Ct. 566 (1981).

Doe v. Koger, 480 F. Supp. 225 (N.D. Ind. 1979).

Southeast Warren Community School Dist. v. Department of Public Instruction, 285 N.W.2d 173 (Iowa 1979).

Stuart v. Nappi, 443 F. Supp. 1235 (D. Conn. 1978).

# Rights of English-Deficient Students

Idaho Migrant Council v. Board of Educ., 647 F.2d 69 (9th Cir. 1981).

United States v. State of Texas, 506 F. Supp. 405 (E.D. Tex. 1981).

Martin Luther King Elementary School Children v. Ann Arbor School Dist., 273 F. Supp. 1371 (E.D. Mich. 1979).

Guadalupe Organization, Inc. v. Tempe Elem. School Dist. No. 3, 587 F.2d 1022 (9th Cir. 1978).

Rios v. Read, 73 F.R.D. 589 (E.D. N.Y. 1977).

Keyes v. School Dist. No. 1, 380 F. Supp. 673 (D. Colo. 1974), *aff'd in part and reversed in part,* 521 F.2d 465 (10th Cir. 1975), *cert. denied,* 423 U.S. 1066 (1976).

Morales v. Shannon, 516 F.2d 411 (5th Cir. 1975).

Otero v. Mesa County School Dist. No. 51, 408 F. Supp. 162 (D. Colo. 1975).

Aspira of New York, Inc. v. Board of Educ. of the City of New York, No. 4002 (S.D. N.Y. 1974).

Lau v. Nichols, 414 U.S. 563 (1974).

Serna v. Portales Municipal Schools, 351 F. Supp. 1279 (D.N.M. 1972), *aff'd,* 499 F.2d 1147 (10th Cir. 1974).

Arvizu v. Waco Independent School Dist., 373 F. Supp. 1264 (W.D. Tex. 1973).

United States v. Texas, 342 F. Supp. 24 (E.D. Tex. 1971), *aff'd,* 466 F.2d 518 (5th Cir. 1972).

# Instructional Grouping Practices and Testing Procedures

Parents in Action for Special Educ. v. Hannon, No. 74-C-3586 (N.D. Ill. 1980).

Larry P. v. Riles, 495 F. Supp. 926 (N.D. Cal. 1979).

Smith v. Dallas County Bd. of Educ., 480 F. Supp. 1324 (S.D. Ala. 1979).

United States v. Gadsden County School Dist., 572 F.2d 1049 (5th Cir. 1978).

Cuyahoga County Ass'n for Retarded Children and Adults v. Essex, 411 F. Supp. 46 (N.D. Ohio 1976).

Lebanks v. Spears, 417 F. Supp. 169 (E.D. La. 1976).

Lemon v. Bossier Parish School Bd., 444 F.2d 1400 (5th Cir. 1971).

Dianna v. State Bd. of Educ., No. C-70-37 RFP (N.D. Cal. 1970).

Stewart v. Phillips, No. 70-119-F (D. Mass. 1970).

Hobson v. Hansen, 269 F. Supp. 401 (D.D.C. 1967), *aff'd sub nom.* Smuck v. Hobson, 408 F.2d 175 (D.C. Cir. 1969).

Moore v. Tangipahoa Parish School Bd., 304 F. Supp. 244 (E.D. La. 1969).

Singleton v. Jackson Municipal Separate School Dist., 419 F.2d 1211 (5th Cir. 1969).

# Compensatory Programs and Desegregation

Robinson v. Vollert, 602 F.2d 87 (5th Cir. 1979), *rehearing denied,* 609 F.2d 1177 (5th Cir. 1980).

Board of Educ. of the City School Dist. of the City of New York v. Harris, 444 U.S. 130 (1979).

School Bd. of Orange County v. Blackford, 369 So. 2d 689 (Fla. App. 1979).

Evans v. Buchanan, 447 F. Supp. 982 (D. Del. 1978).

Reed v. Rhodes, 455 F. Supp. 546 (N.D. Ohio 1978).

Carroll v. Board of Educ., 561 F.2d 1 (6th Cir. 1977).

Milliken v. Bradley, 433 U.S. 267 (1977).

United States v. Columbus Municipal Separate School Dist., 558 F.2d 228 (5th Cir. 1977).

Keyes v. School Dist. No. 1, 380 F. Supp. 673 (D. Colo. 1974), *aff'd in part and reversed in part,* 521 F.2d 465 (10th Cir. 1975), *cert. denied,* 423 U.S. 1066 (1976).

Morgan v. Kerrigan, 401 F. Supp. 216 (D. Mass. 1975), *aff'd,* 530 F.2d 401 (1st Cir. 1976), *cert. denied,* 426 U.S. 935 (1976).

Brown v. Board of Educ. of Chicago, 386 F. Supp. 110 (N.D. Ill. 1974).

United States v. Texas, 466 F.2d 518 (5th Cir. 1971), *cert. denied*, 404 U.S. 1016 (1971).

Plaquemines Parish School Bd. v. United States, 415 F.2d 817 (5th Cir. 1969).

Green v. County School Bd., 391 U.S. 430 (1968).

Lee v. Macon County Bd. of Educ., 267 F. Supp. 458 (M.D. Ala. 1967), *aff'd*, 389 U.S. 215 (1967).

United States v. Jefferson County Bd. of Educ., 372 F.2d 836 (5th Cir. 1966), *aff'd*, 380 F.2d 385 (*en banc*), *cert. denied*, 389 U.S. 840 (1967).

Miller v. School Dist. No. 2, 256 F. Supp. 370 (D. S.C. 1966).

Brown v. Board of Educ., 347 U.S. 483 (1954).

## Instructional Negligence

Doe v. Board of Educ. of Montgomery County, 48 U.S.L.W. 2077 (Md. Cir. Ct., Montgomery County, 1979).

Donohue v. Copiague Union Free Schools, 407 N.Y.S.2d 874 (App. Div. 1978), *aff'd*, 391 N.E.2d 1352 (N.Y. 1979).

Hoffman v. Board of Educ. of the City of New York, 410 N.Y.S.2d 99 (App. Div. 1978), *rev'd*, 424 N.Y.S.2d 376 (Ct. App. 1979).

Smith v. Alameda County Social Services Agency, 153 Cal. Rptr. 712 (Cal. App. 1979).

Peter W. v. San Francisco Unified School Dist., 131 Cal. Rptr. 854 (Cal. App. 1976).

## Competency Testing

Anderson v. Banks, Johnson v. Sikes, 520 F. Supp. 472 (S.D. Ga. 1981).

Debra P. v. Turlington, 474 F. Supp. 244 (M.D. Fla. 1979), *aff'd in part, vacated and remanded in part*, 644 F.2d 397 (5th Cir. 1981).

Wells v. Banks, 266 S.E.2d 270 (Ga. App. 1980).

Brady v. Turlington, 372 So. 2d 1164 (Fla. App. 1979).

Green v. Hunt, No. 78-539 CIV-5 (E.D.N.C. 1979).

Florida State Bd. of Educ. v. Brady, 368 So. 2d 661 (Fla. App. 1979).

# Appendix B

# State Constitutional Provisions Pertaining to the Legislative Duty To Provide for Public Elementary and Secondary Education

## Abridged Constitutional Mandates by State

### Alabama

It is the policy . . . to further and promote the education of its citizens in a manner consistent with its available resources, and the willingness and ability of the individual student, but nothing [herein] shall be construed as creating or recognizing any right to education. . . . Art. 14, § 256 as amended by Amendment 111.

### Alaska

The legislature shall by general law establish and maintain a system of public schools open to all children. . . . Art. 7, § 1.

### Arizona

The legislature shall . . . provide for the establishment and maintenance of a general and uniform public school system. . . . Art. 11, § 1.

### Arkansas

Intelligence and virtue being the safeguards of liberty and the bulwark of a free and good government, the state shall ever maintain a general, suitable and efficient system of free public schools and shall adopt all suitable means to secure to the people the advantages and opportunities of education. Art. 14, § 1.

### California

A general diffusion of knowledge and intelligence being essential to the preservation of the rights and liberties of the people, the Legislature shall encourage by all suitable means the promotion of intellectual, scientific, moral, and agricultural improvement. Art. 9, § 1.

### Colorado

The General Assembly shall . . . provide for the establishment and maintenance of a thorough and uniform system of free public schools throughout the state. . . . Art. 9, § 2.

## Connecticut

There shall always be free public elementary and secondary schools in the state. The general assembly shall implement this principle by appropriate legislation. Art. 8, § 1.

## Delaware

The General Assembly shall provide for the establishment and maintenance of a general and efficient system of free public schools. . . . Art. 10, § 1.

## Florida

Adequate provision shall be made by law for a uniform system of free public schools. . . . Art. 9, § 1.

## Georgia

The provision of an adequate education for the citizens shall be a primary obligation of the state of Georgia, the expense of which shall be provided by taxation. Art. 8, § 1.

## Hawaii

The State shall provide for the establishment, support and control of a statewide system of public schools free from sectarian control. . . . Art. 9, § 1.

## Idaho

The stability of a republican form of government depending mainly upon the intelligence of the people, it shall be the duty of the legislature . . . to establish and maintain a general, uniform and thorough system of public, free common schools. Art. 9, § 1.

## Illinois

The State shall provide for an efficient system of high quality public educational institutions and services. Art. 10, § 1.

## Indiana

Knowledge and learning, generally diffused throughout a community, being essential to the preservation of a free government, it shall be the duty of the General Assembly to encourage, by all suitable means, moral, intellectual, scientific, and agricultural improvement; and to provide . . . for a general and uniform system of common schools, wherein tuition shall be without charge, and equally open to all. Art. 8, § 1.

## Iowa

The General Assembly shall encourage by all suitable means, the promotion of intellectual, scientific, moral and agricultural improvement. Art. 9, 2nd, § 3.

## Kansas

The Legislature shall provide for intellectual, educational, vocational and scientific improvement by establishing and maintaining public schools. . . . Art. 6, § 1.

## Kentucky

The General Assembly shall, by appropriate legislation, provide for an efficient system of common schools throughout the state. § 183.

## Louisiana

The goal of the public education system is to provide learning environments and experiences . . . that are . . . designed to promote excellence in order that every individual . . . may be afforded an equal opportunity to develop to his full potential. The legislature shall provide for the education of the people of the state and shall establish and maintain a public education system. Art. 8, Preamble and § 1.

## Maine

A general diffusion of the advantages of education being essential to the presentation of the rights and liberties of the people . . . to promote this important object . . . it shall be their duty to require the several towns to make suitable provision, at their own expense, for the support and maintenance of public schools. . . . Art. 8, § 1.

## Maryland

The General Assembly shall by law establish throughout the state a thorough and efficient system of free public schools; and shall provide by taxation, or otherwise, for their maintenance. Art. 8, § 1.

## Massachusetts

Wisdom and knowledge, as well as virtue, diffused generally among . . . the people, being necessary for the preservation of their rights and liberties; and as these depend on spreading the opportunities and advantages of education . . ., it shall be the duty of legislatures and magistrates, . . . to cherish the interests of literature and the sciences. . . . Ch. 5, § 2.

## Michigan

Religion, morality and knowledge being necessary to good government and the happiness of mankind, schools and the means of education shall forever be encouraged. The legislature shall maintain and support a system of free public elementary and secondary schools. . . . Every school district shall provide . . . without discrimination as to religion, creed, race, color or national origin. Art. 8, §§ 1 and 2.

## Minnesota

The stability of a republican form of government depending mainly upon the intelligence of the people, it is the duty of the legislature to establish a general and uniform system of public schools. The legislature shall . . . secure a thorough and efficient system of public schools throughout the state. Art. 13, § 1.

## Mississippi

The legislature may, in its discretion, provide for the maintenance and establishment of free public schools for all children between the ages of six (6) and twenty-one (21) years, . . ., and with such grades as the legislature may prescribe. The legislature has the sole power of establishing a free school or schools in each county. . . . Art. 8, §§ 201 and 205.

## Missouri

A general diffusion of knowledge and intelligence being essential to the preservation of the rights and liberties of the people, the general assembly shall establish and maintain free public schools. . . . Art. 9, § 1(a).

## Montana

It is the goal of the people to establish a system of education which will develop the full educational potential of each person. Equality of educational opportunity is guaranteed to each person of the state. The legislature shall provide a basic system of free quality public elementary and secondary schools. . . . It shall fund and distribute in an equitable manner to the school districts the state's share of the costs of the basic . . . system. Art. 10, § 1(1) and (2).

## Nebraska

The legislature shall provide for the free instruction in the common schools . . . of all persons between the ages of five and twenty-one years. Art. 7, § 1.

## Nevada

The legislature shall encourage by all suitable means the promotion of intellectual, literary, scientific, mining, mechanical, agricultural, and moral improvements. . . . Art. 2, § 1.

## New Hampshire

Knowledge and learning, generally diffused through a community, being essential to the preservation of a free government; and spreading the opportunities and advantages of education through the various parts of the county, being highly conducive to promote this end; it shall be the duty of the legislators and magistrates . . . to cherish the interest of literature and the sciences . . .; to countenance and inculcate the principles of humanity and general benevolence, public and private charity, industry and economy, honesty and punctuality, sincerity, sobriety, and all social affections, and generous sentiments among the people. . . . Pt. 2, Art. 83.

## New Jersey

The Legislature shall provide for the maintenance and support of a thorough and efficient system of free public schools for the instruction of all the children in the State between the ages of five and eighteen years. The fund for the support of free public schools . . . and the income thereof, . . . , shall be annually appropriated to the support of free public schools, and for the equal benefit of all the people of the State. . . . Art. 8, § 4(1) and (2).

## New Mexico

A uniform system of free public schools sufficient for the education of, and open to, all children of school age in the state shall be established and maintained. Art. 12, § 1.

## New York

The legislature shall provide for the maintenance and support of a system of free common schools, wherein all the children of this state may be educated. Art. 11, § 1.

## North Carolina

Religion, morality, and knowledge being necessary to good government and the happiness of mankind, schools, libraries, and the means of education shall forever be encouraged. The General Assembly shall provide by taxation and otherwise for a general and uniform system of free public schools, . . . wherein equal opportunities shall be provided for all students. Art. 9, Preamble and § 2.

## North Dakota

A high degree of intelligence, patriotism, integrity and morality on the part of every voter in a government by the people being necessary . . . the legislative assembly shall make provision for the establishment and maintenance of a system of public schools which shall be open to all children of the state. . . . The legislative assembly shall provide for a uniform system of free public schools throughout the state. . . . The legislative assembly shall take such other steps as may be necessary to prevent illiteracy, secure a reasonable degree of uniformity in course of study, and to promote industrial, scientific, and agricultural improvements. Art. 8, §§ 1, 2, and 4.

## Ohio

The general assembly shall make such provisions by taxation, or otherwise, as, with the income arising from the school trust fund, will secure a thorough and efficient system of common schools throughout the state. . . . Art. 6, § 2.

## Oklahoma

The Legislature shall establish and maintain a system of free public schools wherein all the children of the state may be educated. Art. 12, § 1.

## Oregon

The Legislative Assembly shall provide by law for the establishment of a uniform and general system of Common schools. Art. 8, § 3.

## Pennsylvania

The General Assembly shall provide for the maintenance and support of a thorough and efficient system of public education to serve the needs of the Commonwealth. Art. 3, § 14.

## Rhode Island

The diffusion of knowledge, as well as of virtue, among the people, being essential to the preservation of their rights and liberties, it shall be the duty of the general assembly to promote public schools, and to adopt all means which they may deem necessary and proper to secure . . . the advantages and opportunities of education. Art. 12, § 1.

## South Carolina

The General Assembly shall provide for the maintenance and support of a system of free public schools open to all children in the state and shall establish, organize and support such other institutions of learning, as may be desirable. Art. 11, § 3.

## South Dakota

The stability of a republican form of government depending on the morality and intelligence of the people, it shall be the duty of the legislature to establish and maintain a general and uniform system of public schools wherein tuition shall be without charge, and equally open to all; and to adopt all suitable means to secure to the people the advantages and opportunities of education. Art. 8, § 1.

## Tennessee

The State . . . recognizes the inherent value of education and encourages its support. The General Assembly shall provide for the maintenance, support and eligibility standards of a system of free public schools. Art. 2, § 12.

## Texas

A general diffusion of knowledge being essential to the preservation of the liberties and rights of the people, it shall be the duty of the Legislature . . . to establish and make suitable provision for the support and maintenance of an efficient system of public free schools. Art. 7, § 1.

## Utah

The Legislature shall provide for the establishment and maintenance of a uniform system of public schools, which shall be open to all children of the state. . . . Art. 10, §1.

## Vermont

Laws for the encouragement of virtue and prevention of vice and immorality ought to be constantly kept in force, and duly executed; and a competent number of schools ought to be maintained in each town unless the general assembly permits other provisions for the convenient instruction of youth. Ch. 2, § 68.

## Virginia

The General Assembly shall provide for a system of free public . . . schools . . . and shall seek to ensure that an educational program of high quality is established and continually maintained. Standards of quality . . . shall be determined and prescribed from time to time by the Board of Education, subject to revision only by the General Assembly. The General Assembly shall determine the manner in which funds are to be provided for the cost of maintaining an educational program meeting the prescribed standards of quality. . . . Art. 8, §§ 1 and 2.

## Washington

It is the paramount duty of the state to make ample provision for the education of all children residing within its borders, without distinction or preference on account of race, color, caste, or sex. The Legislature shall provide for a general and uniform system of public schools. Art. 9, Preamble and § 2.

## West Virginia

The legislature shall provide, by general law, for a thorough and efficient system of free schools. Art. 12, § 1.

## Wisconsin

The legislature shall provide by law for the establishment of district schools, which shall be as nearly uniform as practicable; and such schools shall be free and without charges for tuition. . . . Art. 10, § 3.

## Wyoming

The right of the citizens to opportunities for education should have practical recognition. The legislature shall suitably encourage means and agencies calculated to advance the sciences and liberal arts. Art. 1, § 23. The legislature shall provide for the establishment and maintenance of a complete and uniform system of public instruction. . . . The legislature shall . . . create and maintain a thorough and efficient system of public schools, adequate to the proper instruction of all youth of the state. . . . Art. 7, §§ 1 and 9.